Active English DISCUSSION

Andrew Finch

2

> *This book is dedicated to Heebon, without whom it could not have been written. Thank you for all the wonderful hints and suggestion, and for all your contributions, especially just being there. you have helped to make this book what it is.*
> ## *Thank you.*

Preface

When we discuss, we use thinking skills such as problem-solving, critical thinking, deduction, inference, reasoning and summarizing. We also express our ideas and opinions simply and clearly, using persuasion, suggestion, agreement and negotiation. *Active English Discussion 2* helps students develop these skills in English, in a cooperative learning environment that focuses on group-work, creativity and mutual respect. Each Unit develops the vocabulary, phrases and techniques needed for discussion and debate, helping students share the ideas, beliefs and values that are important to them.

In order to do this, the eight pages in each Unit follow a similar structure, building the language, ideas and discussion skills step by step. This gradual, student centered approach promotes the informed sharing of facts and opinions that is the essence of true discussion:

Page 1: Pre-reading. Studentsactivate the "reading schema," exploring the topic together before reading, discussing, debating, or making role-playsabout it. These activities are mostly interactive, preparing students for group-work.

Page 2: Topic-reading. This section presents a reading passage about the topic of the Unit, introducing key vocabulary and concepts. Students can listen to this passage on the CD-Rom accompanying the book. Further follow-up reading passages are offered on the Pearson website.
- **Match the Words:** Key words from the passage are presented in a matching format, encouraging students to extend or confirm their store of vocabulary.

Page 3: While-reading: Comprehension and Extension.Students check and expand their knowledge and understanding.
- **Comprehension Check:** These questions help students to review the reading passage in greater detail.
- **Think for Yourself:** These questions invite students to creatively explore the issues in the reading passage.
- **Background Information:** Further information useful for discussion and debate is offered here. This can motivate students to find more facts and figures by themselves.

Page 4: Post-reading: Discussion. Students have sufficient vocabulary and information by now to express their opinions on questions related to the topic of the Unit. However, a useful sub-section isaddedat the bottom of the page:
- **Conversation Strategies:** These gambits offer helpful idioms and phrases to be used in the discussion.

Page 5: Role-Play: Dialogue. Students listen to the dialogue on the CD-Rom and then take on the roles of the characters, exploring the main topic in a conversational, informal manner, before making their own role-plays.
- **Key Words and Expressions:** Idioms and expressions from the dialogue are highlighted and explained.
- **Dialogue Quiz:** These quizzes invite students to discover more about the ideas in the dialogue.

Page 6: Getting Ready. In preparation for the role-plays or debates which appear on page 7 of each Unit, students think of ideas for their role or their side of the debate, using various methods, including brainstorming and outlining. Appropriate phrases and idioms are introduced to help students acquire the language of role-plays and debates.

Page 7: Let's Debate!/Role-play! Groups now perform their role-play or hold a mini-debate, with two teams and a timekeeper. They are now combining information, opinions, key expressions and persuasion strategies, either in real-life role-play or in reasoned debate.
- **Opinion Samples:** These show how students can make role-play dialogues or debate arguments using the phrases from page 6. These samples are either on this or the following page.

Page 8: Reflection and Puzzle Page. The final page of each Unit offers students a chance to reflect on and review their learning. These activities take various forms in each Unit. In some, students are encouraged to reflect on their performance and achievement through self-assessments, surveys, or questionnaires. In others, Opinion Samples are followed by puzzles or riddles related to the topic of the Unit, encouraging students to engage in challenging, but creatively rewarding problem-solving.

Online Follow-up Activities. For teachers and students who want to do access reading, listening, viewing and other activities, suggested links to suitable online resources can be found on www.inkbooks.co.kr/.

In conclusion, I'd like to welcome you to this revised and expanded version of *Active English Discussion 2* and thank you for taking the time to read this preface. I sincerely hope it will provide endless opportunities for holistic development of discussion and debating skills, along with collaboration, respect, and the polite expression of opinions and ideas. Health and peace

Andrew Finch
November 2016

Contents

Preface	4
Who's Who	8

1 Friendship — 9
- Friendship — 10
- Discussion — 12
- Dialogue — 13
- Role-play — 14
- Samples and Review — 16

2 Favorites — 17
- Favorite words — 18
- Discussion — 20
- Dialogue — 21
- Role-play — 22
- Puzzle and Review — 24

3 Movies — 25
- Bollywood — 26
- Discussion — 28
- Dialogue — 29
- Role-play — 30
- Reflect and Review — 32

4 Advice — 33
- Advice from the Oracle — 34
- Discussion — 36
- Dialogue — 37
- Role-play — 38
- Words from the Oracle — 40

5 Confidence — 41
- Self-Confidence — 42
- Discussion — 44
- Dialogue — 45
- Debate — 46
- Let's Debate — 48

6 Healthy Diet — 49
- Healthy Eating — 50
- Discussion — 52
- Dialogue — 53
- Debate Tips — 54
- Let's Begin! — 56

7 Studying Abroad — 57
- Home or Abroad? — 58
- Discussion — 60
- Dialogue — 61
- Debate — 62
- Argument Sample — 64

8 Art and Music — 65
- Art as Therapy — 66
- Discussion — 68
- Dialogue — 69
- Debate Corner — 70
- Let's Debate! — 72

9 Internet Shopping — 73
- Computer Scams — 74
- Discussion — 76
- Dialogue — 77
- Role-play — 78
- Reflection — 80

10 Traffic — 81
- Traffic Blues — 82
- Discussion — 84
- Dialogue — 85
- Debate — 86
- Car Park Puzzle — 88

11 Culture Shock — 89
- Getting to Know You — 90
- Discussion — 92
- Dialogue — 93
- Role-play — 94
- Brainteasers — 96

12 Proverbs — 97
- The Early Bird — 98
- Discussion — 100
- Dialogue — 101
- Debate — 102
- Hidden Proverbs — 104

13 News Media — 105
- Breaking News — 106
- Discussion — 108
- Dialogue — 109
- Role-play — 110
- My Listening Skills — 112

14 Modern Life — 113
- Smart phones — 114
- Discussion — 116
- Dialogue — 117
- Debate — 118
- Reflection — 120

15 Relationships — 121
- Modern Relationships — 122
- Discussion — 124
- Dialogue — 125
- Role-play — 126
- My Discussion Skills — 128

16 Progress — 129
- Save the World — 130
- Discussion — 132
- Dialogue — 133
- Debate — 134
- Save the World Puzzle — 136

17 Konglish — 137
- World Englishes — 138
- Discussion — 140
- Dialogue — 141
- New Languages — 142
- My Conversation Skills — 144

18 The Global Village — 145
- The Global Village — 146
- Discussion — 148
- Dialogue — 149
- Trivia Game — 150
- Review — 152

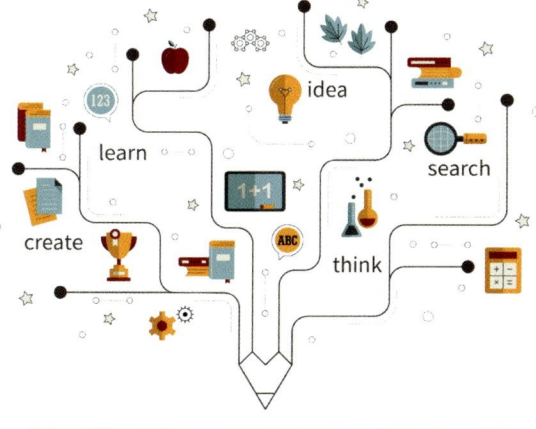

Answer Key — 153

Website: www.inkbooks.co.kr

Who's Who?

Family and Friends

- We're going to meet six people in this book.
- They will talk about the topics in each unit.
- Can you find out who they are?
- ➡ Write their names in the empty spaces.

This is Helen's mother-in-law. She is called _ _ _ _ _ _ _.

Helen's husband is called _ _ _ _ _ _ _ _.

_ _ _ _ _ is Michael's wife.

This is Kevin's friend, Park _ _ _ _ _ _ - _ _ _ _.

Kim _ _ - _ _ _ is Jenny's friend.

Jenny's brother, _ _ _ _ _, is Seung-min's friend.

_ _ _ _ _ is Helen's daughter and Ji-hye's friend.

*You can check the names in the Answer Section at the back of the book.

Unit 1 Friendship

Brainstorming

- How many friends do you have?
- How often do you meet your friends?
- How well do you know your friends?

Task 1
- Exchange books with your partner.
- Ask your partner these questions and write his/her answers.

1 How did you meet your best friend? _____
2 What do you have in common? _____
3 What do you like to do together? _____
4 How often do you meet? _____
5 Have you ever argued? Why? _____
6 What qualities are important to you in a friend? _____
7 Do you find it easy to make friends? Why? Why not? _____
8 Are you a good friend? Why? Why not? _____

Task 2
- Exchange books with your partner.
- Ask your partner the questions below.
- Write his/her answers in the boxes.
- Look at the Answer section and tell your partner what his/her answers mean.

Please tell me ...
1) ... the first number you think of.
2) ... the second number that comes to mind.
3) ... the name of a person of the opposite gender.
4) ... the name of a friend or family member.
5) ... the name of another person (anyone).
6) ... the name of another person (anyone).
7) ... another person of the opposite gender.
8) ... the title of the first song you think of.
9) ... the title of the second song you think of.
10) ... the title of the third song you think of.
11) ... another song.

Friendship

- Read this passage together and listen to track 1.
- While you read, match the words and definitions at the bottom of the page.

 Groups

Friendship goes back to the dawn of history. The earliest known written tale, The Epic of Gilgamesh (c. 2100 BCE), often seen as the first great work of literature, is about the friendship between Gilgamesh, the king of Uruk, and Enkidu, a wild man created by the gods to fight him. Homer told of the friendship of Achilles and Patroclus, in his Iliad (c. 760-710 BCE) and the Hebrew Bible describes the friendship promise made by David, King of Israel, and Jonathan. Furthermore, the philosophers Aristotle and Plato both said friendship was an important characteristic of human beings.

But what is friendship? This might seem to be a strange question at first sight. After all, we all have friends, and we know what friendships mean to us. When we look deeper into this question, however, we find that friendship has many meanings. In the most frequently used meaning, two or more people share knowledge, worth, and affection. They like being together and want whatever is best for each other. Their tastes (food, clothes, music, etc.) are usually similar, and they like doing the same activities. They are sympathetic, honest, and understanding to each other. Most of all, a good friend will give unpleasant advice if necessary, and will share hard times as well as good times. As the saying goes, 'A friend in need is a friend indeed.'

So it might be difficult to put one's finger on the exact meaning, but we can see that friendship is a basic human quality. The Roman scholar Cicero summed it up when he said, 'Life is nothing without friendship.'

Match the words and phrases on the left to the definitions on the right.

at first sight	character or nature
frequently	define; describe
worth	kind; caring; thoughtful
similar	like; resembling
sympathetic	often
dawn of history	seeing for the first time
philosopher	someone who studies ideas about truth
characteristic	special feature
put one's finger on	the beginning of civilization
quality	value; meaning

Further Reading: There are more reading passages at www.inkbooks.co.kr

Comprehension Check

1. How many characteristics of friendship can you find in the reading passage?
2. Who was Enkidu?
3. Is friendship natural, or do we learn it?
4. What will a true friend do in difficult situations?
5. Can you find another word for 'quality' in the passage?
6. Is it easy to define 'friendship'?

Think for Yourself

- [ ] What can you find out about Gilgamesh?
- [ ] What do you know about Achilles?
  Check out google.co.kr or ask.com.
- [ ] What does 'BCE' mean?
  Check out google.co.kr or ask.com.
- [ ] What does 'c.' mean in 'c. 2100 BCE'?
- [ ] What sort of 'unpleasant advice' would a good friend give?
- [ ] What is a 'fair weather friend'?
- [ ] What is a 'false friend'?

Background Information

Have you heard of these types of friendship?

- [ ] **Pen pal, E-pal:** People become friends through writing letters or emails to each other
- [ ] **Internet friendship:** People meet and become friends online
- [ ] **Platonic life-partner:** Two people of either gender become extremely close friends and live together.
- [ ] **Boston marriage:** Two ladies live together in friendship, without male support.
- [ ] **Blood brotherhood:** Two friends swear to help each other for ever and show this by mixing some blood.

Did you know?

- [ ] There is a city in Nebraska, USA, called Friend.
- [ ] There is a university in Kansas, USA, called Friends University.
- [ ] The 'Friends' sitcom ran from 1994 to 2004. It won an EMMY award and was one of the most popular TV series of all time. It has been shown in more than 100 countries.

Discussion Groups

- Talk about the questions below.
- Use the **Conversation Strategies** at the bottom of the page.

1 What makes a good friend?
  ▶ Support your opinion.

2 'Good friends are hard to find.'
  ▶ Do you agree? Why? Why not?

3 What will you do for your friends?
  ▶ Will you lend money?
  ▶ Will you help your friends in hard times?

4 Is friendship more important than honesty?
  ▶ Would you tell a lie for your friend?
  ▶ Why? Why not? Support your opinion.

5 Would you give unpleasant advice to your friend?
  ▶ Why? Why not? Explain your ideas.

6 Can people from different generations be friends?
  ▶ Why? Why not? Explain your ideas.

7 Can people of different genders be good friends?
  ▶ Why? Why not? Explain your ideas.

8 Is it possible for rich and famous people to have good friends?
  ▶ Can money buy true friendship?
  ▶ Why? Why not? Support your opinion.

9 Can parents be friends with their children?
  ▶ Why? Why not? Support your opinion.

Conversation Strategies.

Putting things in sequence:

First of all,	To begin with,
Then,	Furthermore,
Next,	On top of that,
After that,	What's more,
Finally,	In conclusion,

Dialogue

- Listen to Track 2 on the CD-Rom.
- Read the dialogue with your partner.
- Perform the dialogue together.
- Change roles. Perform the dialogue again.

Seung-Min	Hi, Mrs. Brown. How's it going?
Mrs. Brown	Fine, thanks, Seung-min. How about you?
Seung-min	Not bad. Have you seen Kevin?
Mrs. Brown	He left about an hour ago. Didn't he tell you?
Seung-Min	No. We were supposed to meet here.
Mrs. Brown	He went out with his friends. I think they've gone bowling.
Seung-Min	Oh. He must have forgotten our appointment.
Mrs. Brown	Don't worry Seung-min. It's bound to be a misunderstanding.
Seung-Min	If you say so, Mrs. Brown.
Mrs. Brown	Why don't you ring him up and find out?
Seung-Min	I'd rather not. I don't want to disturb him.
Mrs. Brown	Don't be silly. You're one of his best friends.
Seung-Min	I thought so too.
Mrs. Brown	Don't worry. I'm sure there's a simple explanation.

Key Words and Expressions

"How's it going?"
"How are things?"
"What's new?"

"Not bad."
"OK" "So-so."

"It's bound to be …"
"It must be …"

"If you say so."
"I believe you."

"Don't be silly."
"What are you talking about?"
"Be reasonable."

Dialogue Quiz

1. How does Seung-min feel at the end of this dialogue?
2. How does Mrs. Brown feel?
3. Why is Seung-min upset?
4. What advice does Mrs. Brown give him?
5. Why doesn't Seung-min want to ring Kevin?
6. What do you think will happen next?

Let's Make a Role-play! Us Groups

- This role-play is about friendship. It is based on the Dialogue on page 13.
- You can perform this role-play or you can make your own role-play about friendship.

❶ Choose your role (Seung-min, Kevin, Mrs. Brown or Jenny).
❷ Read your role-card and the opinion sample on it.
❸ These opinion samples are to help you make your role-play.
❹ There are some more on page 16.
❺ Think about what you will say in the role-play.
❻ Write your ideas on the next page.

Seung-min: First of all, Kevin is a good friend, but he is forgetful. He gets carried away with what he is doing and forgets the time. On top of that, he forgets our appointments. I don't know what to do. I don't want to keep calling him up and reminding him. It might seem as if I don't trust him. I think we need to talk, face to face. I need to give him some friendly advice.

Kevin: To begin with, I like Seung-min, but he's a bit of a worrier. Yes, of course I forget a few appointments, but so what? Good friends understand each other and forgive each other. Anyway, I thought I'd invited Seung-min to come bowling with my other friends. I wanted to introduce them to him. It looks like one of us got it wrong.

Mrs. Brown: Oh dear! I don't like to see these misunderstandings. I know that Kevin is forgetful, but he means well. It's just that he's a little thoughtless. When he wants to do something, he doesn't think about other people. He just does it. What's more, he's hurting Seung-min, who is the best friend he's ever had. I think I'd better sit them both down and talk to them about it.

Jenny: Kevin is a good brother, but he can be too offhand at times. What's more, I don't like to see him taking Seung-min for granted. I'm not sure what I can do, but I'm sure something can be worked out. Perhaps I can bring up the subject next time we are all together. I'd like to help them sort this out. After all, that's what sisters are for!

You can use these ideas in your role play, or you can make your own ideas.

My Notes

- Fill in the mind-map with your ideas for the role-play.

First of all: _____

Next: _____

Furthermore: _____

On top of that: _____

Finally: _____

Let's begin! Groups

- Use these phrases when you perform your role-play.
- There are some opinion samples on the next page.

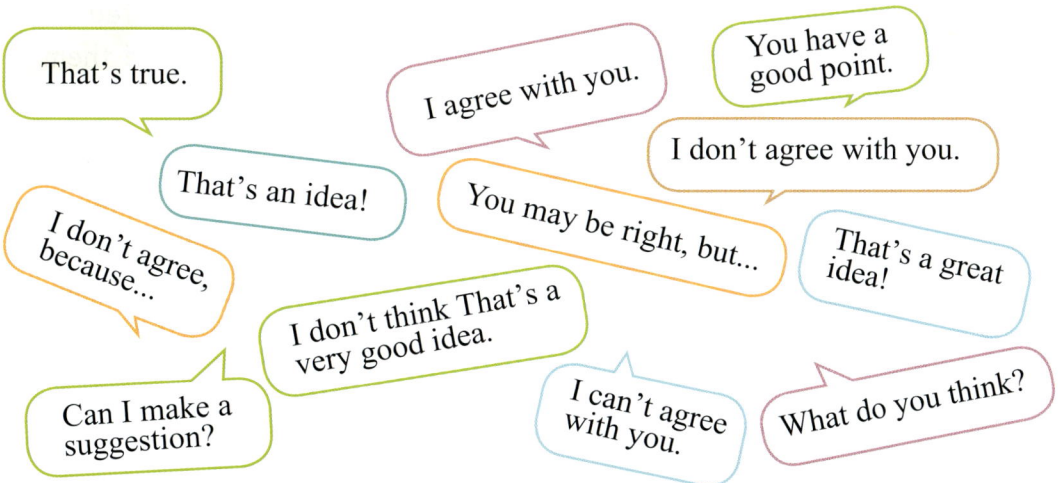

When you have finished, complete this final statement about your discussion.

We have agreed that Kevin will _____.

We have also agreed that Seung-min will _____.

Signed: 1. _____ 2. _____ 3. _____ 4. _____

Friendship 15

What Do You Think? Us Groups

Track 7 and 8

- Here are some more opinion samples about friendship.
- Which ideas do you agree with? Which ideas do you disagree with?

Opinion 1: A really good friend is worth more than money. He or she will support you and help you through thick and thin. In fact, I can't imagine my life without friends being there to share the good times and the bad times. They help me believe in myself and pick me up when I feel down. Of course, it's not easy to find good friends, but once you have found them, they are a treasure forever.

Opinion 2: I'm not sure about friendship. It sounds very good in theory, but how often does it happen in real life? I've been hurt a number of times by fair-weather friends, and I don't want to be hurt again. As the saying goes, 'Once bitten, twice shy.' People often seem to be good friends, until you really need them, and then you can't see them for dust. I'm better off taking care of myself.

Reflect and Review

- How did you do in this Unit?

How was your speaking (pages 9, 12, 15)?			
Great	Good	OK	Could be better
How was your reading (pages 10, 13, 14)?			
Great	Good	OK	Could be better
How was your team work with your group and your partner?			
Great	Good	OK	Could be better
Did you learn any new words, idioms, or phrases? What were they?			
How about looking at the online activities for this Unit? www.inkbooks.co.kr			

Unit 2 Favorites

Brainstorming

- Do you have any favorite music, movies, clothes, or TV shows?
- What is your favorite pastime?
- How about your favorite actor or actress?

Task 1 • Choose 10 of these words and write them in the Favorite things boxes.

actor	color	flower	politician	sports person
animal	computer game	ice-cream	season	singer
bird	day of the week	Internet site	shop	teacher
book	drink	mountain	song	tree
city	fashion	pastime	sport	TV show

Favorite things	What/Who?	Why?
1		
2		
3		
4		
5		
6		
7		
8		
9		
10		

Task 2
- Ask your partner about the 10 things you have entered above.
- What is your favorite color? Who is your favorite actor?
- Write his/her answers in the **What/Who?** boxes.

Task 3
- Ask your partner Why? For example: Why is green your favorite color?
- Write his/her answers in the **Why?** boxes.

Favorite words

- Read this passage together and listen to track 9.
- While you read, match the words and definitions at the bottom of the page.

Do you have a favorite place, a favorite time of day, or a favorite pastime? When you browse the Internet, do you bookmark your favorite sites? Do you have any favorite words? This might sound like a funny question, but there are many favorite words that people use, even though they are not in any dictionaries.

An example is 'spinter.' This is the time between winter and spring, when the weather is very changeable. As you can see, it is made from the first two letters of 'spring' and the last five letters of 'winter.' You can probably guess what 'sprummer' means and you won't be surprised to learn that 'snirt' means snow that has become dirty. How about 'furgle'? This is a different type of word. It comes from the sound you make when you feel in your pockets for money or keys. Another type of favorite new word is 'fumb.' This sounds like 'thumb,' so it's easy to see that it refers to the thumb on our foot - the big toe.

Your Design / Shutterstock.com

Nobody is sure where these new words come from. They become popular because they are interesting and easy to use. Then, after some time, they are included in dictionaries and become part of the language. Other new words are actually invented by individuals. For example, the word 'googol' was invented in 1920 by Milton Sirotta (1911-1981), the nephew of an American mathematician. It refers to a 1 followed by 100 zeros and was changed to 'Google' when it became the name of a popular search engine.

Language is always changing. New words are made and old, unused words disappear. What do you think? Can you make some new favorite words? Why not give it a try?

Match the words and phrases on the left to the definitions on the right.

pastime	a program that finds matches
bookmark	fade; vanish; pass out of sight
popular	generally liked; well-known
invent	hobby; spare time activity
search engine	make; create
disappear	make an attempt; experiment
give it a try	save a location

Further Reading: There are more reading passages at www.inkbooks.co.kr

Comprehension Check

1. How can you save the location of favorite Internet sites?
2. What do you think 'finter' means?
3. Which words have been combined to make 'snirt'?
4. Can you find another word for 'big toe' in the passage?
5. Where do new words come from?
6. When do new words get included in dictionaries?
7. How old was Milton Sirotta when he invented the word 'Googol'?
8. What happens to words that nobody uses any more?

Think for Yourself

- ☐ Why do people have favorite words?
- ☐ Why aren't these words in the dictionaries yet?
- ☐ Do you know any interesting new words?

- ☐ How about making a new word now?
  My new word is: _____.
  It means: _____.

Woot!
(An expression of joy or excitement)

Chillax
(Chill out/relax)

Confuzzled
(Confused and puzzled at the same time)

404
(Someone who has no idea. From the WWW error message '404 not found')

Noob
(A new member of an online community)

Staycation
(A stay-at-home holiday)

Background Information

Did you know?

- ☐ Napoleon's favorite color was green.
- ☐ Justin Timberlake's favorite color is baby blue.
- ☐ Johnny Depp's favorite color is black.
- ☐ Angelina Jolie's favorite color is also black.
- ☐ Hillary Clinton's favorite TV show is 'House of Cards.'
- ☐ Will Smith's favorite words are: 'Yeah, Uh, What, Haha.'
- ☐ Chris Daughtry's favorite band is Live.
- ☐ The actor Chevy Chase's favorite book is *Moby Dick*.
- ☐ London was the favorite city for tourists in 2015.
- ☐ California Institute of Technology was the top university in the world in 2015/16 (Times Higher Education).
- ☐ Lionel Messi (Barcelona, Argentina) was the world's favorite soccer player in 2015/16.
- ☐ The best movie of all time according to rottentomatoes.com is 'The Wizard of Oz', 1939.
- ☐ The world's favorite song is Queen's 'We Are The Champions'.

Discussion Us Groups

- Talk about the questions below.
- Use the **Conversation Strategies** at the bottom of the page.

1 What is your favorite color (or animal or food)?
  ▶ Why? Explain your choice.

2 What is your favorite book (or character from literature)?
  ▶ Why? Explain your choice.

3 What is your favorite movie (or television program)?
  ▶ Why? Explain your choice.

4 Who is your favorite movie star (or teacher)?
  ▶ Talk about him or her.

5 What is your favorite day of the week (or time of the day)?
  ▶ Why? Explain your choice.

6 What is your favorite season?
  ▶ Talk about your choice.

7 Do you have a favorite folktale, fairy tale or story?
  ▶ What is it? Describe it to everybody.

8 Do you have a favorite piece of music (or song)?
  ▶ What is it? Sing it to everybody.

9 Do you have a favorite Internet site?
  ▶ What is it? Why is it your favorite?

10 What is your favorite childhood memory?
  ▶ Describe it to everyone.

Conversation Strategies.

Asking a question:

| Can I ask you a question? |
| Can I ask you something? |
| Do you mind if I ask you something? |
| Excuse me. |
| Can you tell me … ? |
| I'd like to know … |
| Do you mind if I ask … ? |

➡ What's your favorite childhood memory?
➡ … your favorite song or piece of music.

Indecision:

| Let me see. |
| Let me think. |
| I'm not sure. |
| I can't tell you. |
| It's hard to say. |
| I don't really know. |
| I've never really thought about it. |

Dialogue

- Listen to Track 10 on the CD-Rom.
- Read the dialogue with your partners.
- Perform the dialogue together.
- Change roles. Perform the dialogue again.

Key Words and Expressions

"No problem."
"Don't worry."
"It's not a problem."

sleeping over
staying overnight at a friend's house

genre
type

"way before your time"
"long before you were born"

(Kevin and Grandma Brown are watching a movie on TV, when Ji-hye enters.)

Ji-hye	Hi, Kevin. What're you watching?
Kevin	Hi, Ji-hye. It's one of my favorite movies, *Titanic*.
Grandma Brown	Hello Ji-hye.
Ji-hye	Oh, hello Grandma Brown. I didn't see you.
Grandma Brown	No problem, Ji-hye. Are you looking for Jenny?
Ji-hye	Yes, that's right. She's sleeping over at my house tonight.
Kevin	She'll be down soon. She's just getting ready.
Grandma Brown	Do you like *Titanic*, Ji-hye?
Ji-hye	Hmm. Not really. I prefer romantic comedies, like *My Sassy Girl*.
Kevin	What's your favorite genre, grandma?
Grandma Brown	Let me see. I love romances, like *Gone with the Wind*.
Ji-hye	Gone with the what? I've never heard of it.
Kevin	Me neither.
Grandma Brown	Don't worry. It was way before your time. *(Jenny comes down the stairs.)*
Ji-hye	Ah, here's Jenny. Time to go.
Grandma Brown	Have a good time.
Kevin	Enjoy!

Dialogue Quiz

1. Why doesn't Ji-hye say 'Hello' to Grandma Brown at first?
2. Where is Jenny during most of this dialogue?
3. Do the Brown family live in a bungalow (one-storey house)?
4. What is Ji-hye's favorite movie genre?
5. Has Kevin heard of *Gone with the Wind*?
6. What sort of movie is it?

Let's Make a Role-play! Groups

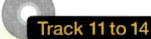
Track 11 to 14

- **Situation:** The Brown family are having dinner together. They are talking about their favorites. They all have different opinions and they tell each other about them.

1. Choose your role (Michael, Helen, Jenny or Kevin).
2. Read your role-card and the opinion sample.
3. Listen to Tracks 11 to 14 on the Audio CD-Rom.
4. Think about what you will say in the role-play.
5. Write your ideas on the mind-map on the next page.

Jenny: Here is your opinion sample:

My favorites tend to come and go. If I like a new song, for example, I listen to it all the time, until I'm fed up with it. After that I forget all about it. You could say my favorites are always changing. I'm always excited by the latest fashion, but only for a while. It's the same with pop music, movie stars, and everything else. It's nice to have favorites, but it's even nicer to keep moving on.

Michael: Here is your opinion sample:

My favorite time of the day is when I come home from work. I can sit down and relax. Then I like to watch my favorite TV show or maybe listen to my favorite music. Perhaps if there is nothing on TV, I will read one of my favorite books. Of course, everyone has different likes and dislikes. I know not everyone shares mine. As the saying goes, 'One man's meat is another man's poison.'

Kevin: Here is your opinion sample:

I haven't really thought about my favorites before, so it's hard to say which movies or books I like more than others. Let me think. In fact, I'm not sure that I have any favorites at all. I like eating, but I don't have any special favorite food. I like listening to music too, but only when I'm studying. On the other hand, I can't stand coffee. Perhaps that's my non-favorite drink!

Helen: Here is your opinion sample:

My favorite time of day is in the morning, after Michael has gone to work and Jenny and Kevin have gone to school. Then I can get on with my job as a webpage designer. I work from home, so I am in my favorite place - my study - all the time. I am very lucky. I have my favorite people - my family - round me. I am doing my favorite job and I can work whenever I want.

My Mind-map

- Fill in the mind-map with your ideas for the role-play.

Food / Drink	Book / Music	Color / Animal

Favorites

Time of day / Day of the week	Childhood memory	Actor / Movie

Let's begin! Groups

- Use these phrases and the ones on page 20 when you perform your role-play.
- Also use the opinion samples (page 22) and your ideas (My Mind-map).

- Tell us about your favorites.
- How about you?
- Let me think.
- To tell the truth, ...
- That reminds me.
- What do you think?
- Frankly speaking, ...
- Off the top of my head...
- Now you mention it, ...
- Now I come to think of it, ...
- It's funny you should ask.

Favorites 23

Time to Think! Us Groups

- Look at the clues below and find who lives in each house.
- Write their name and their favorite color under their house.

❶ John, Mary, Peter and Jane have different favorite colors.
❷ Their favorite color is not the same as their house color.
❸ John's favorite color is red. The other man's favorite color is blue.
❹ Mary does not live in the blue house. Her favorite color is yellow.
❺ Jane lives at the end of the road. Her favorite color is green.

Name				
Favorite color				

*The solution is in the Answer Section at the back of the book.

Reflect and Review Me

- How did you do in this Unit?

How was your speaking (pages 17, 20, 23)?			
Great	Good	OK	Poor (I will do my best.)
How was your reading (pages 18, 21, 22)?			
Great	Good	OK	Poor (I will do my best.)
How was your team work with your group and your partner?			
Great	Good	OK	Poor (I will do my best.)
Did you learn any new words, idioms, or phrases? What were they?			
How about looking at the online activities for this Unit? www.inkbooks.co.kr			

Unit 3 Movies

Brainstorming

- When did you last see a movie?
- What was it called?
- What movie genre (type) was it?

Task 1

- How many movie titles (English or Korean) can you think of?
- Write them in their genre boxes. Can you fill every box?

Action	Comedy	Romantic comedy	Musical	Science fiction
Documentary	Crime	Fantasy	Spy	Sports
Animation	Horror	Historical	Romance	Thriller

Task 2

- Choose one movie genre. Ask 12 people for their favorite movie in that genre:
- Use the phrases on page 20. For example:
  - ☐ Excuse me. What's your favorite documentary?
  - ☐ Can I ask you a question? What's your favorite historical movie?
  - ☐ Let me see. I think it's …… It's hard to say. Maybe ……

My chosen genre:				
People's favorite movies in this genre are:	1	2	3	4
	5	6	7	8
	9	10	11	12

Bollywood

- Read this passage together and listen to track 15.
- While you read, match the words and definitions at the bottom of the page.

 Groups

Surely, everybody has heard of Hollywood. It is the place where big-budget American movies are made. Most people have also heard of the Cannes, Berlin, and Venice Film Festivals. However, how many people have heard of Bollywood?

Believe it or not, Indian cinema is the biggest film industry in the world. There are more than 30 film production companies, making 1,600 movies every year. 14 million people watch Bollywood (Bombay + Hollywood) movies each day, including viewers in Asia, Russia, Africa and the Middle East. Even in the west, where Asian communities are growing fast, Bollywood movies are becoming popular.

Most Bollywood films are musicals and the soundtrack is often released before the movie, in order to attract more people. Indians love to forget their worries by watching movies, so they like to see bright, colorful films with famous actors and actresses singing and dancing on the screen. In the popular Masala (mixture) genre, many elements appear over and over again. You can expect to see young lovers, angry parents, comedy, action, corruption, love-triangles, kidnapping, long-lost relatives, changes in fortune, and unbelievable coincidences.

A typical Bollywood feature film lasts for 3 hours and has an intermission in the middle. Why don't you watch one when you have the chance? It could be an unforgettable experience!

Match the words and phrases on the left to the definitions on the right.

big-budget	a group of people with similar interests
cinema	capturing someone for money
community	costing lots of money
musical	made available to the public
soundtrack	movie that contain many songs
released	movie theater; movie industry
genre	music and songs from a movie
kidnapping	two things happening at the same time
coincidence	type; classification; category

Further Reading: There are more reading passages at www.inkbooks.co.kr

Comprehension Check

1. Which three film festivals are mentioned in the passage?
2. How many Indian cinema movies are made each year?
3. How did Bollywood get its name?
4. Are Bollywood movies shown only in India?
5. What genre are most Bollywood movies?
6. Can you find the name of a special Bollywood genre?
7. Can you find another word for 'film industry' in the passage?

Think for Yourself

- [ ] How many film festivals can you think of?
- [ ] Have you ever watched a Bollywood movie?
- [ ] Have you ever watched movies that were not made in Hollywood or Korea?
- [ ] What do you think of the Korean film industry?

Background Information

Did you know?

- [ ] 1919. The first Korean movie was called "Uirijeok Gutu".
- [ ] 1923. The first Korean silent film, "Plighted Love Under the Moon", was directed by Yun Baek-nam.
- [ ] 1935. The first Korean sound film, "The Story of Chunhyang", was directed by Lee Myeong-woo.
- [ ] 1949. The first Korean color film, "The Women's Diary", was directed by Hong Seong-gi.
- [ ] 1974. The Korean Film Archive (KFA) started.
- [ ] 1996. The Busan International Film Festival (BIFF) started. This was the first international film festival in Korea.
- [ ] 2000. The Jeonju International Film Festival started.
- [ ] 2001. The New York Korean Film Festival started.
- [ ] 2004. The Los Angeles Korean International Film Festival started.
- [ ] 2004. "Silmido" and "Taegukgi" were the first Korean films to sell 10 million tickets.
- [ ] 2007. Korean actress Jeon Do-yeon won the Cannes best actress award for her performance in "Secret Sunshine".
- [ ] 2010. "Poetry" won the Best Screenplay Award at the Cannes Film Festival
- [ ] 2012. Kim Ki-duk's "Pietà" became the first Korean film to win the top prize at the Venice Film Festival.

Discussion Groups

- Talk about the questions below.
- Use the **Conversation Strategies** at the bottom of the page.

1 What is your favorite movie genre?
▶ Explain your choice to the others.

2 What do you think of Hollywood movies?
▶ Explain your opinion.

3 What do you think of Korean movies?
▶ Explain your opinion.

4 Are movies art, or are they entertainment (or both)?
▶ Support your opinion.

5 What do you think about movie copyright?
▶ Is it OK to make copies of DVDs?
▶ Is it OK to download movies from the Internet?

6 Do you think movie stars make too much money?
▶ Support your opinion.

7 Would you like to be a movie star or director?
▶ Why? Why not? Explain your ideas.

8 Do you think some movies are too violent?
▶ Why? Why not? Support your opinion.

9 Do movies have a harmful effect on children?
▶ Support your opinion.

10 What do you think about movie censorship?
▶ Explain your opinion.

Conversation Strategies.

Asking a question:

What about … How about … Have you thought of …	▶ going to see a movie?
Why don't we … Perhaps we could … Maybe we could …	▶ see a movie?

Indecision:

In my opinion, To my mind, As I see it, I feel that … It seems to me that …	▶ that's not a bad idea.

Dialogue

- Listen to Track 16 on the CD-Rom.
- Read the dialogue with your partners.
- Perform the dialogue together.
- Change roles. Perform the dialogue again.

Key Words and Expressions

earlier showing
the previous showing of the movie

sit down for a bit
sit down for a short while

take the weight off my feet
give my feet a rest; sit down

Chick Flick
a movie aimed at girls and young women

(Grandma Brown, Mrs. Brown and Jenny are waiting in the lobby of a movie theater.)

Jenny	Mum, this was a cool idea of yours.
Mrs. Brown	Thanks, Jenny. I thought you'd like it.
Grandma Brown	What time does the movie start? We've been here for ages.
Mrs. Brown	Don't worry, mum. The doors will open soon.
Jenny	We have to wait for the earlier showing to finish.
Grandma Brown	I think I'll sit down for a bit and take the weight off my feet.
Mrs. Brown	Ah, the people are coming out now.
Jenny	And we can go in. Come on, Grandma. I'll help you up.
Grandma Brown	Thank you, Jenny.
Mrs. Brown	You know, I can't remember the last time we went to a movie theater.
Jenny	Me neither. But I'm really glad we're doing it now.
Grandma Brown	What are Michael and Kevin doing? Why couldn't they come?
Jenny	Didn't you hear, Grandma? They've gone fishing together.
Mrs. Brown	Yes. They both love fishing.
Jenny	And it gives us the chance to watch a Chick Flick.
Grandma Brown	What's that, Jenny?
Jenny	It's the sort of romantic comedy that guys hate.
Mrs. Brown	That sounds good. Let's sit back and enjoy!

Dialogue Quiz

1. What was the cool idea?
2. What are they waiting for?
3. Why aren't Mr. Brown and Kevin with them?
4. Do they often go to the movies together?
5. What sort of movie are they going to watch?

Let's Make a Role-play! Groups

- **Situation:** There are 4 movies showing at the local movie theater: An action movie, a romance, an animation, and a comedy. Jenny, Kevin, Ji-hye and Seung-min are deciding what movie to watch. You will make a role play of their conversation.

❶ Choose your role (Jenny, Kevin, Ji-hye or Seung-min).
❷ Read your role-card and the opinion sample.
❸ Listen to Tracks 17 to 20 on the Audio CD-Rom.
❹ Think about what you will say in the role-play.
❺ Write your ideas on the mind-map on the next page.

Jenny: Here is your opinion sample:

I really want to watch the romantic movie. I don't want to see fighting or killing, or even a silly comedy. Animations don't turn me on either. I want to see lovers overcoming all the odds. A nice love story makes me feel good, even if it makes me cry. It also makes me think about life. I want to have my own romance some day. I hope everyone will agree to watch the romantic movie.

Kevin: Here is your opinion sample:

I want to watch the action movie. I really like watching fights and car chases. Everyone knows they're not real, but they are exciting all the same. I don't like comedies. They are just silly. As for romances! They are all the same. The two lovers get married at the end and live happily ever after. I don't mind animations, but they're not my favorite genre. I hope everyone will agree to watch the action movie.

Ji-hye: Here is your opinion sample:

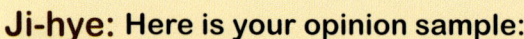

I want to watch the comedy. I like to have a good laugh. I don't want to watch killing or fighting. Even in a romance there are too many sad scenes. I want something lighthearted. I want everyone to release their stress and worries. Comedies are good for health. They help us to relax and laugh at ourselves as well as at the actors. If I have my way we will all agree to watch the comedy.

Seung-min: Here is your opinion sample:

I love watching animations. They are often historical stories or fantasy stories. But they are always exciting. They take us into the world of make-believe. We can forget our worries for a while and watch the heroes doing things that humans cannot do. Comedies and romance movies are so boring and action movies are too predictable. So I hope everyone will agree to watch the animation.

My Ideas

- Make notes about what you will say in the role-play.

First of all, ...
_____
_____
_____
_____

Second, ...
_____
_____
_____
_____

Third, ...
_____
_____
_____
_____

Finally, ...
_____
_____
_____
_____

Let's begin! Groups

- Make your role-play. Use the role-cards on page 30, the phrases on page 28, the ideas that you wrote on this page, and the phrases below.

On the one hand ...
To sum up, ...
On the other hand ...
First of all, ...
In conclusion ...
Second, ...third, ...finally, ...
I'd just like to say that ...
I see your point, but ...
I think that ...
I see what you mean.
Can I say something?

Movies 31

Reflect and Review

- How are your English speaking skills? Try this self-assessment to find your level.

Level	Description	
Basic	I use basic words and phrases.	✓
	I use simple grammar and sentence patterns.	
	I use phrases that I have remembered. I pause a lot.	
	I can ask and answer questions about myself.	
	I can use basic connectors like 'and' or 'then'.	
Upper Basic	I use basic sentences in simple situations.	
	I can use simple grammar correctly, with some mistakes.	
	I can make myself understood, using short phrases.	
	I can answer questions, but it is difficult to keep talking.	
	I can use connectors like 'and', 'but' and 'because'.	
Intermediate	I can talk about hobbies, interests and current events.	
	I can use common grammar and sentence patterns.	
	I can talk for reasonable amounts of time.	
	I can have a conversation on familiar topics.	
	I can link short phrases into longer sentences.	
Upper Intermediate	I can give descriptions and express my opinions.	
	I do not make many mistakes and I correct them when I do.	
	I can talk for some time without hesitating.	
	I can begin conversations and keep them going.	
	I can link my ideas well.	

- What do you think about your level? How can you improve your speaking skills?

I need to _____.

I hope to _____.

I want to _____.

I will _____.

Unit 4 Advice

Brainstorming

- Can you give advice to your best friend?
- Can you listen to advice from your best friend?
- What is the best advice you ever received?

Task 1 — Groups
- Make an Advice Game using the two boards on this page.
- **Board A** is the problem board. **Board B** is the answer board.
- Look at the **Conversation Strategies** on page 36 for advice phrases.

study	exercise	diet	date	hard	fat
grades	\multicolumn{4}{c}{**Board A: What should I do?**}		bored
home work	father	job	sleep	unhappy	school

get some exercise	get more sleep	see a doctor	watch a movie	???	say what you think
???	\multicolumn{4}{c}{**Board B: Why don't you …?**}		eat healthy food
study more	ask your teacher for help	Listen to music	???	do your best	cycle to school

Here are some ideas:
1. Student A: Start anywhere on Board A. Throw the die and move round Board A.
2. Make a sentence with your word and add *What should I do?* (p. 36)
3. Student B: Start anywhere on Board B. Throw the die and move round Board B.
4. Give advice to Student A, using the words on Board B and the phrases on p. 36.
5. If you land on ???, give your own advice.

Continue, with everyone going round Boards A and B, asking and giving advice.

Advice from the Oracle

- Read this passage together and listen to track 21.
- While you read, match the words and definitions at the bottom of the page.

 Groups

The citizens of ancient Greece thought that immortal gods controlled their fate. Furthermore, they believed that the gods spoke to humans through oracles. So if the Greeks wanted to find out what was in store for them, they had to consult these divine oracles at places like the temple of Apollo at Delphi. In fact this sanctuary was so important that it was known as the 'omphalos', or navel, of Greek civilization. People came from all over the Greek world to ask about their plans and receive an answer from the oracle.

There were often long queues of people waiting to ask their questions of the priestess at Delphi. However, they had to be careful about the answer, since it often had many meanings. For example, King Croesus (595-546 BCE) asked whether he should go to war against the Persian Empire. The oracle replied 'If Croesus goes to war he will destroy a great empire.' Croesus thought this advice was a good omen and went into battle. Unfortunately, Cyrus the Great (576-530 BCE) destroyed his forces and took him captive. Cyrus ordered Croesus to be burned alive, but he called out to Apollo, asking to be rescued. A sudden shower of rain put out the fire and he was saved.

When Cyrus heard what the oracle had told Croesus, he sent him to Delphi to find out why he had been betrayed. The oracle told him that it had spoken only the truth. A great empire had indeed been destroyed by Croesus - his own empire. This story tells us that when we ask for advice we should think carefully about the answer!

Match the words on the left to the definitions on the right.

immortal	a place where people ask questions to a god
fate	a sacred place; a place of shelter
in store	a sign of something that will happen in the future
consult	about to happen; future happenings
divine	ask for advice
oracle	belly button; hollow area in the middle of the stomach
sanctuary	destiny; something that controls the future
navel	living forever
omen	relating to a god

Further Reading: There are more reading passages at www.inkbooks.co.kr

Comprehension Check

1. How could ancient Greeks talk to the gods?
2. What is an oracle?
3. What does 'omphalos' mean?
4. Why should people be careful about the oracle's answer?
5. How old was Croesus when he died?
6. Who was the leader of the Persian empire?
7. Was the oracle's advice correct?

Michael Paschos / Shutterstock.com

Think for Yourself

- [ ] Where is Delphi?
- [ ] What do you think BCE means?
- [ ] Croesus was king of Lydia. Where was this?
- [ ] What do you know about Greek civilization?
- [ ] Do you know any famous Greeks?

Background Information

Did you know?

1. The oracle at Delphi told Laius, the king of Thebes, that he would be killed by his son, so he killed all his male children.
2. However, one son was saved. His name was Oedipus. Why don't you check out this myth on Wikipedia?
3. The ancient Greek empire started about 4,000 years ago.
4. According to legend, the Greeks captured Troy by hiding inside a wooden horse. You can check out 'Trojan Horse' on Google.com.
5. The Greeks invented theater. Only men and boys could be actors. They all wore masks, which showed whether they were happy or sad.
6. The Greeks started the Olympics in 776 BCE. The winners got a circle of leaves to put on their heads.
7. The Greeks have their own alphabet. The first three letters are Alpha: A,α; Beta: B,β; Gamma: Γ,γ.
8. Democracy started in Greece.
9. Famous Greeks include Plato, Aristotle, Archimedes, Pythagoras and Alexander the Great.
10. Greece is the largest producer of olives in the world.

Discussion Groups

- Talk about the questions below.
- Use the **Conversation Strategies** at the bottom of the page.

1. **Where do you go to get good advice?**
   ▶ Why? Explain your thoughts.

2. **What advice would you give to your children?**
   ▶ Why? Explain your ideas.

3. **What advice would you give to your parents?**
   ▶ Why? Explain your ideas.

4. **What advice would you give to the president of your country?**
   ▶ Why? Give your reasons.

5. **If you could go back in time, what advice would you give to yourself?**
   ▶ Why? Tell everyone about it.

6. **If you see a friend in a difficult situation, can you give advice, even if it is unpleasant?**
   ▶ Why? Why not? Support your opinion.

7. **Do you listen to your parents when they give you advice?**
   ▶ Why? Why not? Explain your opinion.

8. **Do you ever watch TV advice shows (Oprah, etc.)?**
   ▶ Why? Why not? What do you think of them?

9. **Do you ever read the Advice Column in newspapers or magazines?**
   ▶ Why? Why not? What do you think of them?

Conversation Strategies.

Asking for advice:	Giving advice:	Receiving advice:
A) I don't know what to do. A) What can I do? A) What should I do? A) What do you think? A) Can you help me? A) What would you do in my place?	B) If I were you, I'd … B) In your place, I'd … B) Why don't you …? B) How about … ing? B) Have you thought of … ing? B) You could always …	A) That's a good idea. A) That's interesting. A) I hadn't thought of that! A) You could be right. A) What a great idea!

Dialogue

- Listen to Track 22 on the CD-Rom.
- Read the dialogue with your partner.
- Perform the dialogue together.
- Change roles. Perform the dialogue again.

(Mr. Brown and Kevin are fishing together.)

Mr. Brown	Well, Kevin, what d'you think?
Kevin	It's great, dad. I'm really glad I came.
Mr. Brown	So am I. It's nice to get away.
Kevin	Right. Just the two of us.
Mr. Brown	It's so quiet and peaceful.
Kevin	Right.
Mr. Brown	Can I ask you something, now we're alone?
Kevin	Of course, dad. Go ahead.
Mr. Brown	Is anything troubling you?
Kevin	Why do you ask, dad?
Mr. Brown	You seem very quiet these days, and …
Kevin	I know. I'm getting bad grades.
Mr. Brown	What is it? Is there any way we can help?
Kevin	Thanks, but it's my problem. I'll sort it out.
Mr. Brown	We're always here for you, Kevin. Just ask.
Kevin	(*Excitedly*) Wow! I think I've caught a big one. Quick, dad, help me pull it in!

Key Words and Expressions

get away
go somewhere different; forget about daily cares and stress

"It's my problem."
"I can't ask you about it."
"It's very personal."

"I'll sort it out."
"I will find the solution myself."

"We're always here for you."
"We will always support you."

Dialogue Quiz

1. What are Kevin and Mr. Brown doing?
2. Where are the other members of the family? (Look in Unit 3, page 29.)
3. Why does Mr. Brown want to be alone when he asks Kevin his question?
4. What do we know about Kevin's problem?
5. Mr. Brown says 'We're always here for you.' Who does 'We' refer to?

Let's Make a Role-play! Groups

- **Situation:** The friends are playing an advice game. They are taking their problems to the oracle at Delphi. You will play the game on the next page. But first …

① Choose your role (Jenny, Ji-hye, Seung-min, Kevin).
② Read your role-card and listen to your opinion sample.
③ There are more opinion samples on page 40.
④ Think about what you will say in the role-play.
⑤ Jenny, Seung-min, Kevin: Write your ideas on the next page.
⑥ Ji-hye: Look at the answers on page 40.

Jenny: Here is your opinion sample:

I will ask the oracle three questions. First of all, I want to know the next step I should take in my life. Second, I want to know which career is best for me. Third, I want to know how to find true love. These are the most important questions for me right now. I hope the oracle will tell me what to do. I know it's just a game, but I'm going to ask these questions anyway.

Seung-min: Here is your opinion sample:

If I'm allowed to ask three questions, my first question will be 'Can I have three more questions.' However, if the oracle says 'No', then I only have two questions left. I think first of all I will ask how to improve my health. I have been a little sick lately and I need to know what to do. Second, I want to know how to make friends. I have three good friends already, but I want to know how to make many more.

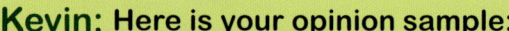

Kevin: Here is your opinion sample:

So I have three questions to ask the oracle. Let me see. First of all I will ask about my grades. How can I get better grades? Second, I want to know how to talk to my parents. I don't think they understand me, but I don't know what to say to them. Third, I want to ask about myself. What do I need to change about myself? How can I become a better person? That will do for now.

Ji-hye: Here is your opinion sample:

I am the priestess of the oracle at the temple of Apollo at Delphi. I will give answers to Jenny, Seung-min and Kevin. However, my answers will be interesting. They will have to think about them carefully. I will speak in a flat voice, like a priestess. I will say 'Who are you?' 'Why have you come to the temple of Apollo?' 'What is your question?' Then I will give them their answer. I like being a priestess!

You can use these ideas in your role play, or you can make your own ideas.

My Ideas Me

- Jenny, Seung-min and Kevin: Decide on your questions. What will you ask the oracle?

My first question

_____

_____

My second question

_____

_____

My third question

_____

_____

Let's begin! Us Groups

- Jenny, Seung-min and Kevin: Ask the oracle your questions.
- Ji-hye: Choose any answers from the next page (page 40).
- Everyone: Use the conversation strategies on page 36.
- Finally: Talk about your questions and answers together.
- Use the opinion samples on page 38 and page 40.
- Here is a sample role-play to give you some ideas:

Ji-hye: Who are you?
Jenny: My name is Jenny Brown.
Ji-hye: Why have you come to the temple of Apollo?
Jenny: I want to ask a the oracle a question.
Ji-hye: What is your question?
Jenny: My question is ..… What should I do? Can you help me?
Ji-hye: The oracle says 'Why don't you ….?'
Jenny: I hadn't thought of that. Thank you. Goodbye.
Ji-hye: Who are you?
Seung-min: I am Park Seung-min

…………………….. (Continue with Seung-min and Kevin.)

Reflect and Review

- Ji-hye: Choose any of these proverbs when you answer a question.
- Any answer is OK. The others have to figure out what it means.

Look before you leap.	When the going gets tough, the tough get going.	Don't put all your eggs in one basket.
When in Rome, do as the Romans.	Two wrongs don't make a right.	Honesty is the best policy.
No man is an island.	Fortune favors the bold.	Don't count your chickens before they hatch.
There's no place like home.	The early bird catches the worm.	Better late than never.
Actions speak louder than words.	You can lead a horse to water but you can't make it drink.	There's no time like the present.
Absence makes the heart grow fonder.	The grass is always greener on the other side of the hill.	Two heads are better than one.
Good things come to those who wait.	You can't judge a book by its cover.	Practice makes perfect.

Opinion Samples

Tracks 27 and 28

- Here are two more samples to give you some ideas.

Opinion 1: I hate it when people give advice without being asked. They say 'If I were you ...' and they expect me to listen. They even think that they are helping me. Who do they think they are? How I live my life is none of their business. These people love to give me advice, but if I try to give them some, they think I'm rude. 'Don't do what I do. Do what I say.' That's how they think. In my opinion, people should keep their advice to themselves.

Opinion 2: I think one of the most difficult things in the world is giving advice to a friend. The next most difficult thing is receiving advice from a friend. When you like someone, you don't want to hurt him or her in any way. But you also want what's best for your friend. Sometimes we have to give unpleasant advice in order to stop bad things happening. This is what friendship is about. We have to tell the truth to each other, even if it hurts!

Unit 5 Self-confidence

Brainstorming

- Are you a confident person? Do you believe in yourself?
- Does confidence help in learning English?

Task 1
- Look at the pictures below. What are these people feeling? How are they acting?
- Choose from the words below and write them in the empty boxes:

angrily	generously	jealously	noisily	rudely	strongly	in a friendly way
confidently	gently	kindly	politely	sadly	sweetly	in a scared way
energetically	happily	nervously	quietly	shyly	weakly	in a tired way

*Suggested answers are in the Answer Key, at the back of the book.

Task 2 Feelings Game

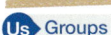 Groups

- Student A: Choose a sentence below. Then perform it, using a word from Task 1.
  For example: Walk to the door **happily**, or close your book **angrily**, or stand up **weakly**.

Stand up.	Smile.	Open the door.	Shake someone's hand.
Sit down.	Sigh.	Close the door.	Walk to the door.
Open your book.	Yawn.	Close your book.	Bow to the teacher.

- Everybody: Can you guess which word Student A has chosen?

Self-Confidence 41

Self-confidence

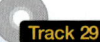

- Read this passage together and listen to track 29.
- While you read, match the words and definitions at the bottom of the page.

 Groups

> One important key to success is self-confidence.
> An important key to self-confidence is preparation. (Arthur Ashe)

Self-confidence is important in every part of life, including learning English. We need to take risks when communicating in a new language, and if we are anxious or nervous this can be very hard. Confident learners, on the other hand, are not afraid to make mistakes, since they know that they are essential for learning. As the saying goes, 'The most successful people make the most mistakes.' Confident people inspire others to believe in them and this leads to success. In contrast, people who lack confidence often lose self-esteem and become trapped in a vicious circle. But how can we become more confident? Here are some suggestions:

1. Stop thinking negatively and be positive at all times. For example, instead of saying 'I can't …,' say 'I will … .'
2. Start believing in ourselves. After all, if we don't believe in ourselves, who will? As the first man to climb Mount Everest (Sir Edmund Hillary) said, 'It is not the mountain we conquer but ourselves.'
3. Follow Roger Federer's advice when he says, 'I believe in old-school hard work.'

In other words, everyone can learn how to be confident. There is no royal road to language learning, but we can make it easier by trusting our abilities and never giving up. Perhaps we should leave the last word with Henry Ford: 'Whether you think you can or you think you can't - you're right.'

Match the words on the left to the definitions on the right.

key to …	a cycle of (bad) events that repeats itself
take risks	beat; control; win over
anxious	easy path
essential	encourage; produce; motivate
inspire	necessary; fundamental; important
vicious circle	solution; answer
conquer	take chances; experiment
old-school	traditional
royal road	worried; nervous; frightened

Further Reading: There are more reading passages at www.inkbooks.co.kr

Comprehension Check

1. Why do language learners need self-confidence?
2. 'The most successful people make the most mistakes.' What does this mean?
3. What does 'vicious circle' mean?
4. What are three methods of becoming self-confident?
5. What does 'There is no royal road to language learning' mean?
6. Can you find another word for 'self-confidence' in this passage?
7. What does 'Whether you think you can or you think you can't - you are right' mean?

Think for Yourself

- [ ] Do you know any confident people?
- [ ] What makes them confident?
- [ ] How does this help them?

Background Information

Here are some quotations about self-confidence:

- [ ] If a voice inside you says, 'You cannot paint,' then you must paint. Then that voice will be silent. (Vincent van Gogh)
- [ ] Success comes in cans, not can'ts. (Anonymous)
- [ ] Put your future in good hands - your own. (Anonymous)
- [ ] I am not a has-been. I am a will-be. (Lauren Bacall)
- [ ] Confidence comes not from always being right but from not fearing to be wrong. (Peter T. Mcintyre)
- [ ] You have to expect things of yourself before you can do them. (Michael Jordan)
- [ ] In theory, bees can't fly. But bees don't know that, so they go on flying anyway. (Mary Kay Ash)
- [ ] Your chances of success in anything can always be measured by your belief in yourself. (Anonymous)
- [ ] Self-confidence is the memory of success. (Anonymous)
- [ ] Success breeds success. (Anonymous)

Discussion Groups

- Talk about the questions below.
- Use the **Conversation Strategies** at the bottom of the page.

1 Why do people lack self-confidence?
   ▶ Explain your opinion.

2 What are your 'Tips for Becoming Self-confident'?
   ▶ Tell your group members about them.

3 Have you ever seen 'Self-help' books in a book store?
   ▶ What do you think of them?
   ▶ Why do people read Self-help books?

4 What is the difference between confidence and arrogance?

5 Can psychiatrists help people who lack self-confidence?
   ▶ Explain your opinion.

6 Would you go to a psychiatrist or a therapist?
   ▶ Why? Why not? Support your opinion.

7 If you could be happy, successful, wealthy, or confident, which one would you choose?
   ▶ Why? Explain your reasons.

8 Is it possible to be successful without self-confidence?
   ▶ Why? Why not? Explain your ideas.

9 Who is the most confident person you know?
   ▶ Talk about that person.

Conversation Strategies.

Giving an opinion:		Generalizing:	
In my opinion, Personally, As for me, If you ask me, As far as I'm concerned, From my point of view,	self-confidence is more important than anything else.	Generally speaking, In general, On the whole, As a rule, Usually, In most cases,	no-one would disagree with you on that.

Dialogue

- Listen to Track 30 on the CD-Rom.
- Read the dialogue with your partners.
- Perform the dialogue together.
- Change roles. Perform the dialogue again.

Key Words and Expressions

soap opera
TV drama series shown in weekly episodes

"Grades aren't everything."
"There are more important things in life than getting good grades."

"Take it easy."
"Relax." "Don't worry." "Calm down."

(Mr. and Mrs. Brown [Michael and Helen] are watching TV in the living room.)

Michael	Can I change the channel, Helen?
Helen	Why, Michael? This is my favorite soap opera.
Michael	But it's so boring. Anyway, there's a big game on tonight.
Helen	Can't you watch the replay tomorrow?

(Seung-min enters, looking anxious.)

Michael	Hello, Seung-min. Are you looking for Kevin?
Seung-min	Actually, I'd like to talk to you both, if that's OK.
Helen	Sit down, Seung-min. *(She turns off the TV.)* How can we help?
Seung-min	I'm really worried, Mrs. Brown, and I don't know what to do.
Michael	What do you mean?
Seung-min	My grades are poor, I can't make new friends, and I can't get on the football team. My parents are so disappointed in me!
Helen	I'm sure they're not, Seung-min. They love you.
Michael	That's right. Grades aren't everything.
Seung-min	But they want me to go to Harvard, and …
Helen	Calm down, Seung-min. Take it easy. Let's talk about it.
Seung-min	*(30 minutes later)* Thank you so much. I feel much better now.
Helen	Don't mention it. And remember – believe in yourself!
Michael	Right. *(to Helen)* Can we watch the football now?

Dialogue Quiz

1. What are Mr. and Mrs. Brown watching on TV?
2. What does Mr. Brown want to watch?
3. Why does Seung-min want to talk with Mr. and Mrs. Brown?
4. Why can't he talk with his parents about his problems?
5. What advice do you think Mr. and Mrs. Brown give to Seung-min?
6. How does Seung-min feel at the end of the dialogue?

Let's Debate!

- In this Unit we will begin to debate.
- Debating is a more formal way of discussing.
- Debating uses conversation strategies and role-play skills.

If I Ruled the World

1. Make a circle of up to 8 people.
2. Speaker 1: Give your name and say what you would do if you ruled the world.
3. Speaker 2: Repeat what speaker 1 said, then disagree, give your name and say what you would do if you ruled the world.
4. Speaker 3: Repeat what speakers 1 and 2 said, then disagree, give your name and say what you would do if you ruled the world.
5. Continue until everyone has said what they would do.
6. Start again. Here are some more topics:
   - If I were amazingly rich, I would …
   - If I could live anywhere, I would live in …
   - If I could visit anywhere, I would visit …
   - If I could be a famous person, I would be …

- When you disagree, use the phrases on pages 44 and 47.
- Here is an example:

Student A: My name is George. If I ruled the world, I would stop all wars.

Student B: If George ruled the world, he would stop all wars. I disagree on the whole. My name is Mary and if I ruled the world I would end poverty.

Student C: If George ruled the world, he would stop all wars and if Mary ruled the world she would end poverty. I can't agree. My name is Eugene and if I ruled the world I would make everyone play soccer.

Debate Corner Us Groups

1. In your group, choose one of the statements (motions) below.

> 1. Self-confidence can be improved by positive thinking.
> 2. Homework should be banned.
> 3. University education should be free.
> 4. Cosmetic surgery should be banned.

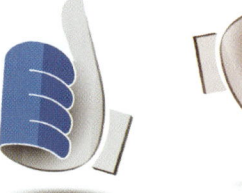

2. Choose one pair of people (Pro) to agree with your motion.
3. The other pair (Con) will disagree with it.
   - Pro Pair: Write three reasons for agreeing with the motion, plus your conclusion.
   - Con Pair: Write three reasons for disagreeing with the motion, plus your conclusion.

First of all, ...
_____
_____
_____

Furthermore, ...
_____
_____
_____

Next, ...
_____
_____
_____

In conclusion, ...
_____
_____
_____

4. Use these phrases when you debate (next page).

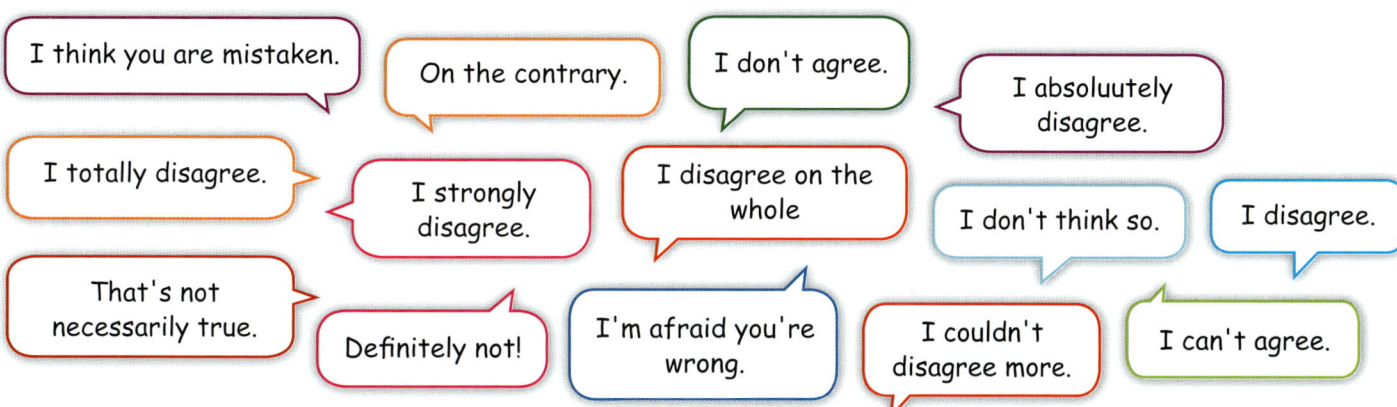

Self-Confidence 47

Let's Begin! Groups

- Pro Pair, Student 1: Explain your three reasons.
- Con Pair, Student 1: Explain your three reasons.
- Pro Pair, Student 2 : Disagree with the Con Pair and give your conclusion.
  Use the phrases on page 47.
- Con Pair, Student 2: Disagree with the Pro Pair and give your conclusion.
  Use the phrases on page 47.

Track 31 to 34

▶ Here is a sample debate on the topic 'Self-confidence can be improved by positive thinking.'

Pro Speaker 1: First of all, I'd like to say that my partner and I agree with this proposition. We believe that self-confidence can be improved by positive thinking. I will give you three reasons. First, positive thoughts help us to believe in ourselves. Second, this belief helps us to succeed. Third, this success gives us confidence. We should start to believe in ourselves first.

Con Speaker 1: My partner and I strongly disagree and we will show you why this motion is wrong. To start with, positive thinking can be empty. We have to have something to be positive about. Next, this means doing our best at all times and working hard. Furthermore, it's no use just having positive thoughts. If they don't lead to success we will be even more unhappy than we were at the beginning.

Pro Speaker 2: I totally disagree with Con Speaker 1. I'm afraid she is very wrong. To begin with, she hasn't told us about negative thoughts. They can make us lose our self-esteem. Second, they lead us into a vicious circle. Third, we often believe negative thoughts, even when we know they are wrong. In conclusion, I ask everyone here to accept the motion. You know it is correct.

Con Speaker 2: Pro Speakers 1 and 2 are obviously mistaken. I cannot agree with them. They don't understand confidence at all. As Con speaker 1 said, we have to have something to be confident about. That means working hard and doing our best at all times. There is no royal road to confidence. To sum up, I hope everyone will reject the motion that self-confidence can be improved by positive thinking.

Unit 6 Healthy Diet

Brainstorming

- Food is very important for life, so there are many food idioms in English.
- Look at this crossword together. Can you solve all the clues?

Task 1 • Food Idioms

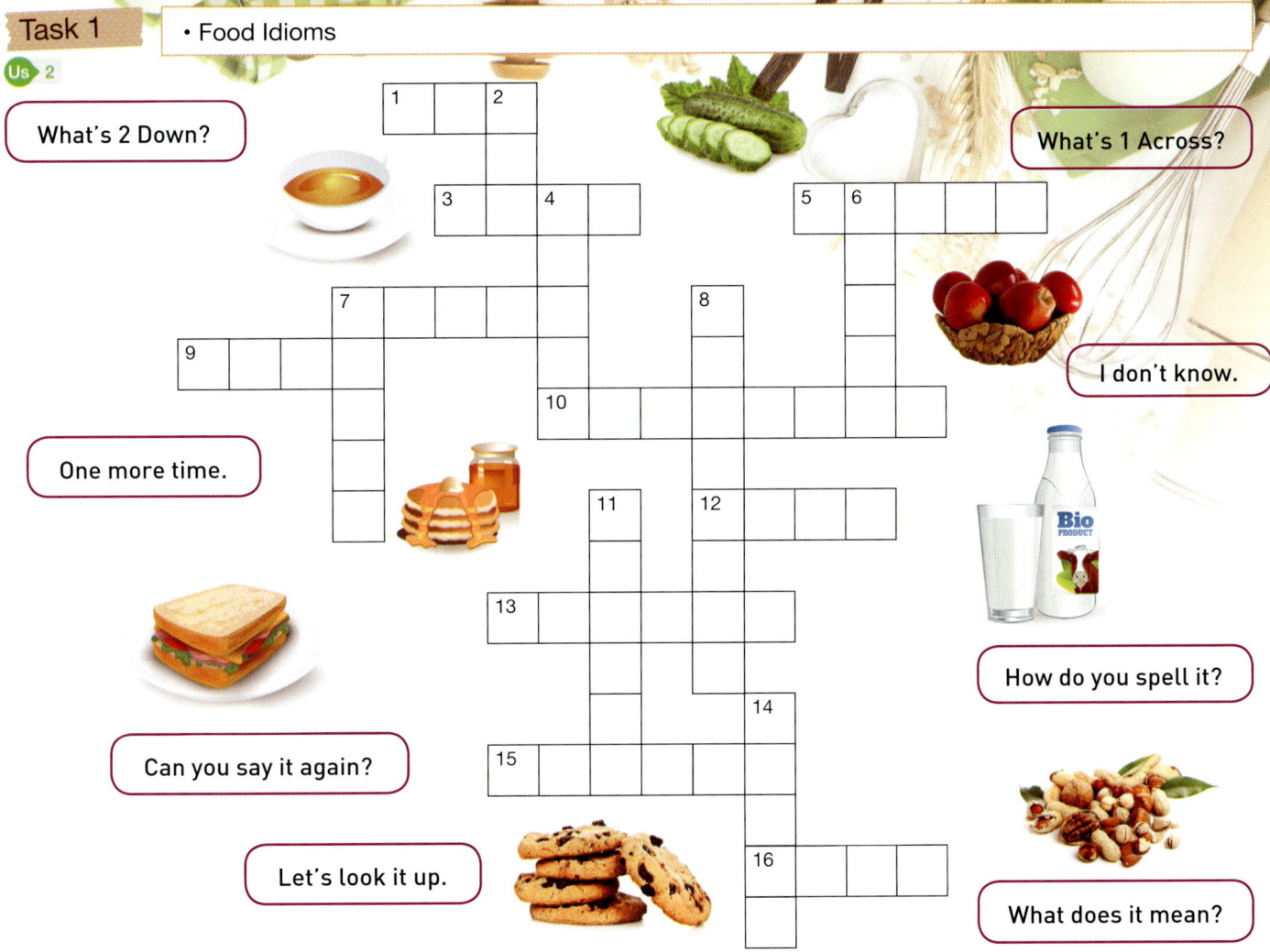

Across

1. I'm afraid you'll have to _____ your words.
3. You should take his words with a pinch of _____.
5. It makes my mouth _____.
7. Who brings home the _____ in your family?
9. It's easy. It's a piece of _____.
10. They are selling like _____.
12. It's no use crying over spilt _____.
13. Don't try to _____ me up!
15. She is one smart _____.
16. I'm _____ about classical music!

Down

2. Horror movies are not my cup of _____.
4. There's no such thing as a free _____.
6. He is the _____ of my eye.
7. What's the problem? Spill the _____.
8. She is as cool as a _____.
11. Don't be a couch _____.
14. You're full of _____ today!

*The answers are in the Answer Key, at the back of the book.

Healthy Diet 49

Healthy Eating

- Read this passage together and listen to track 35.
- While you read, match the words and definitions at the bottom of the page.

Track 35

 Groups

Fijians used to think that a plump, curvy body was the height of beauty. That was before TV came to the island, in 1995. Now, as a result of watching programs mainly from the USA, 3 out of every 4 teenage girls in Fiji think they are overweight. Our society has become obsessed with food and dieting, and many people have eating disorders as a result.

Despite this infatuation with losing weight, The World Health Organization (WHO) has reported that there were 1.9 billion overweight people and 600 million obese people (39% and 13% of the world's adult population) in 2014. Furthermore, the number of obese people doubled from 1980 to 2014.

One reason for this situation is that people are eating more fatty and sugary food. Another is that they are not getting as much exercise as they used to. One third of the average American diet consists of junk foods: soft drinks, sweets, desserts, alcoholic drinks and salty snacks. These increase obesity and can lead to diabetes, heart disease and even cancer. TV ads for junk food are part of the problem, with their unrealistically thin women and muscular men. They are often aimed at children and are much more frequent than ads for nutritious foods.

Losing weight isn't just about eating less. It's about eating and drinking healthy foods: fresh grains, vegetables, fruits, water and milk. And don't forget exercise: jogging, swimming, cycling – anything is OK! Even a 30-minute walk each day will give your heart the exercise it needs.

Match the words on the left to the definitions on the right.

Fijians	a disease which makes people eat too much or too little
plump	a strong love for someone or something
overweight	a sugar disorder in humans
obsessed	chubby; round
eating disorder	dependent; devoted to; hooked on
infatuation	extremely fat in a way that is unhealthy
obese	food which has little nutritional value
junk food	not sensible; not as in real life
diet	people who live in Fiji, in the Pacific Ocean
diabetes	the food that people usually eat; a strict eating plan
unrealistic	too heavy; weighing more than normal people

Further Reading: There are more reading passages at www.inkbooks.co.kr

Comprehension Check

1. How has the popular view of beauty changed in Fiji?
2. Why do many Fijian girls think they are fat?
3. What do the letters 'WHO' stand for?
4. How many people were overweight in 2014?
5. What percent of the world's adult population were obese in 2014?
6. What problems can obesity lead to?
7. How are TV ads for junk food unrealistic?
8. What is the best way to lose weight and stay healthy?

Think for Yourself

- [ ] What sort of food is healthy?
- [ ] What sort of food is unhealthy?
- [ ] What is junk food?
- [ ] What is fast food?
- [ ] Do you exercise regularly?

Background Information

Did you know?

- [ ] Breakfast is the most important meal of the day.
- [ ] Fish is called 'brain food.' It also reduces the risk of heart disease, cancer, and Alzheimer's disease.
- [ ] Fruit juices are often high in calories.
- [ ] Low-fat, high-calcium dairy foods may burn off fat.
- [ ] Olive oil fights arthritis.
- [ ] Chicken Nuggets contain twice as much fat as hamburgers.
- [ ] 12 to 19-year-old boys in the USA drink about 868 cans of soft drinks per year. Girls drink about 651 cans per year.
- [ ] A typical strawberry milkshake contains about 50 additives, which make the 'strawberry' taste.
- [ ] 46% of adults are overweight or obese in Canada.
- [ ] The number of obese children in Canada has tripled in 20 years.
- [ ] 7 million women and 1 million men in the USA suffer from eating disorders.
- [ ] Many processed foods have a higher level sugar than coke.

Discussion Groups

- Talk about the questions below.
- Use the **Conversation Strategies** at the bottom of the page.

1 What makes a healthy diet?
 ▶ Explain your opinion.

2 What is the strangest food you have ever eaten?
 ▶ Tell everyone about it.

3 Do you count the calories when you eat?
 ▶ Why? Why not? Give your reasons.

4 What do you think about organic food?
 ▶ explain your ideas.

5 What do you think about junk food and fast food?
 ▶ Support your opinion.

6 Is it OK to kill animals for food?
 ▶ Why? Why not? Explain your opinion.
 ▶ What do you think of vegetarians?

7 What do you think about genetically modified (GM) food?
 ▶ Why do you think that way?

8 Is it OK to eat beef from countries that have had Mad Cow Disease?
 ▶ Why? Why not? Support your opinion.

9 Is it OK to eat chickens and ducks from countries that have had bird flu?
 ▶ Why? Why not? Support your opinion.

10 What do you think about dieting?
 ▶ Is it healthy? Is it fashionable?
 ▶ Does it lead to eating disorders?

Conversation Strategies.

Considering things:

When you think that … Considering that … When you remember that … Bearing in mind that … Given that …	health is so important,

Trying to understand:

I can't see why … it beats me why … I don't see why … it's weird how … it's beyond me why …	people take it for granted.

Dialogue

- Listen to Track 36 on the CD-Rom.
- Read the dialogue with your partner.
- Perform the dialogue together.
- Change roles. Perform the dialogue again.

(Seung-min knocks on the front door. Grandma Brown opens it.)

Grandma Brown	Seung-min! What brings you here so early?
Seung-min	Hello, Grandma Brown. I've come for Kevin. We're going on a school trip today.
Grandma Brown	That's nice. Where are you going?
Seung-min	To the new History Theme Park. Have you heard of it?
Grandma Brown	Yes, that rings a bell. How long will you be gone?
Seung-min	We'll be back about 5 p.m.
Grandma Brown	Don't you have any lunch to eat?
Seung-min	No problem. They have fast food shops there.
Grandma Brown	You mean hamburgers and hot dogs?
Seung-min	Of course. And soda, sweets and ice cream.
Grandma Brown	What do you mean? They're no good for young bodies!
Seung-min	Sorry, Grandma Brown. I was just joking. My lunch is in my backpack.
Grandma Brown	You had me worried there. Ah. Here's Kevin. Have a good time, both of you.

Key Words and Expressions

"What brings you here so early?"
Why are you visiting at this time of day?

"That rings a bell."
"That sounds familiar."

"No problem."
"Don't worry."
"It's not a problem."

"You had me worried."
"I was worried because of you."

Dialogue Quiz

1. What time of day do you think it is?
2. Where is Seung-min going today?
3. Who is he going with (in addition to Kevin)?
4. What will they eat at lunchtime?
5. Why was Grandma Brown worried?
6. Do you think Kevin has his lunch with him?

Debate Tips Groups

- This is our second debate, so let's look at some debate tips.
- Talk About these tips together.
- When you debate in later Units, use this page as a checklist.

> Don't raise your voice. Improve your argument.

> In all debates, let truth be thy aim, not victory.

> It is better to debate a question without settling it than to settle a question without debating it.

✔ My Debate Tips

1 Prepare well in advance.
2 Wear appropriate clothes.
3 Look confident, even when you are nervous.
4 Make eye contact with the audience.
5 Know your facts and figures.
6 Make a strong opening statement.
7 Use positive body language.
8 Look as if you are enjoying yourself. Smile.
9 Use repetition to make your point.
10 Use rhetorical questions.
11 Sound interesting. Look as if you are interested.
12 Make a strong closing point.
13 Support your partner with non-verbal language.
14 Work together as a team.

- Stand straight, head up, shoulders back.
- 'Statistics show that …'
- 'I have a dream.'
- 'Education, education, education.'
- 'How long can we put up with this?'
- 'Why hasn't anything been done about this?'
- 'We cannot afford to ignore global warming.'
- 'United we stand, divided we fall.'
- Nodding, facial expressions.

Debate Corner

- In your group, choose one of the motions below and write it on the next page.

1. You are what you eat.
2. Dieting is unhealthy and dangerous.
3. TV ads for junk food should be banned.
4. It is wrong to kill animals for food.

- Choose one pair of people (Pro) to agree with your motion.
- The other pair (Con) will disagree with the motion.
  ▸ Pro speakers: Write three reasons for agreeing with the motion, plus your conclusion.
  ▸ Con speakers: Write three reasons for disagreeing with the motion, plus your conclusion.

First of all, …

Furthermore, …

Next, …

In conclusion, …

- Now look at these phrases. You will use them in the debate (next page).
- These phrases help you state your argument and make your point.

Healthy Diet 55

Let's Begin! Us Groups

- Let's begin the debate!
- write your debate motion here (page 55):

- Pro-Speaker 1: Stand up and begin the debate.
- Don't forget the Debate Tips on page 54.

| **Pro Speaker 1:** Explain your three reasons (page 55). Use the phrases on pages 52 and 55. | **Con Speaker 1:** Explain your three reasons (page 55). Use the phrases on pages 52 and 55. | **Pro Speaker 2:** Disagree with the Con Pair and give your conclusion. Use the phrases on pages 52 and 55. | **Con Speaker 2:** Disagree with the Con Pair and give your conclusion. Use the phrases on pages 52 and 55. |

Argument Samples

- Here are two argument samples for Pro Speaker 1 and Con Speaker 1.
- They are based on motion number 2 (page 55): Dieting is unhealthy and dangerous.
- Listen to Tracks 37 and 38 on the CD-Rom while you read the samples.
- You can use these as a model for your speech if you wish.

Track 37

Pro Speaker 1: I will speak in favor of the motion. First of all, I don't need to remind you that society is obsessed with dieting and being thin. Second, no-one would disagree that this puts terrible pressure on young people. They think that nobody will like them unless they're thin as a rake, so they go on harmful diets. Third, statistics show that over 50% of young people go on a diet and that this often results in eating disorders. Considering these facts, I can't see why this infatuation with physical appearance continues. It is obvious that it is harming our future citizens.

Track 38

Con Speaker 1: I will speak against the motion. First of all, everyone would agree that if you want to be cool these days, you've got to go on a diet and get a fashionable, thin body. Just look at the TV ads and the women's magazines. It is common knowledge that all the models and actors are thin. Second, it is common sense that teenagers shouldn't go on diets, since their bodies are still growing, but there's really no choice. All the best pop stars and movie actors have great bodies and we all want to be like them. Third, dieting is not dangerous if you do it properly. Without doubt, a careful diet can help you get a great body.

Unit 7 Studying Abroad

Brainstorming
- Why do people study abroad?
- How can they find the best places to study?

Task 1
- Here is a world map. Look at it together.
- Write the names of universities in the boxes.
- You can do an Internet search to find the universities.
- Look for the keywords: World Universities.

North America
(USA, Canada)

Europe, Middle East, Russia

South America, Africa

Asia, Australia, New Zealand

Studying Abroad 57

Home or Abroad?

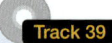

- Read this passage together and listen to track 39.
- While you read, match the words and definitions at the bottom of the page.

Us Groups

South Korean students have been some of the most internationally mobile students in recent years, their numbers peaking at 262,465 in 2011. However, the Bank of Korea has reported a significant decline in spending by Koreans studying abroad. By 2014, they spent 26% less than the $5 billion of 2007. It appears that the global economic crisis of 2008 was a turning point for many who could no longer afford to study in the US or the UK.

Because of a weakening economy and improved English education at home many students have decided to stay in Korea, while others have settled for more affordable universities abroad. The USA is still the favorite destination, with 30% of Korean international students, but their number is falling and is almost matched by those studying in China. The Philippines is also a popular destination, showing a 52% increase in Korean students from 2013 to 2014.

Of course, there are many advantages to studying abroad. Not only can students learn in an English-speaking environment, but they can also experience a different culture, meet other international students and expand their intellectual horizons.

On the other hand, studying English in Korea is much easier than it used to be. Students can now watch TV programs in English, study English online, watch movies in English, and even study intensively in English Villages. Many young people are finding that it is not necessary to go abroad, unless they wish to study their major or do graduate studies.

Match the words on the left to the definitions on the right.

mobile	a difficult or dangerous situation
peaking	able to move around
significant	arriving at the highest level
decline	decrease
billion	equalled
crisis	increase; get larger; widen
affordable	one thousand million
matched	very important; noticeable
expand	way of thinking; perspective
intellectual horizons	within one's price range

Further Reading: There are more reading passages at www.inkbooks.co.kr

Comprehension Check

1. When did the number of Korean students studying abroad peak?
2. How much did Korean students spend on studying abroad in 2007?
3. Why was 2008 a turning point?
4. Why have many Korean students decided to stay in Korea?
5. Where is the favorite destination for international Korean students?
6. What country increased its number of Korean students by 52% in 2013-14?
7. What are four advantages of studying abroad?
8. How can Korean students study English in Korea?
9. What is the conclusion of the passage?

Think for Yourself

- ☐ How many Korean students were studying abroad last year?
  (Do an Internet search for 'Korean students studying abroad.')
- ☐ Which university would you choose if you were to study abroad?
- ☐ Would you go as an undergraduate, an exchange student, or a graduate student?

Background Information

Did you know?

- ☐ In 1960, there were 48,000 international students in the USA.
- ☐ In 2014-15, there were 974,926 international students in the USA. The main countries of origin of these students were China (31%), India (11.6%) and South Korea (7.7%).
- ☐ The National Universities with the largest number of international students in the USA in 2014-15 were: Florida Institute of Technology (33%), New School, New York (32%), Illinois Institute of Technology (30%), University of Tulsa (27%) and Lynn University (23%).
- ☐ In 2013-14, 304,467 US students studied abroad, mostly in the UK, Italy, Spain and France.
- ☐ In April 2015, there were 91,332 foreign students studying in Korea. The government aims to attract 200,000 international students by 2020, through the Study Korea 2020 Project.
- ☐ 45% of foreign student graduates extend their visas to work in the same area as their college or university in the USA.
- ☐ In a survey of 420 international students in 2015, 78% thought that studying abroad improved their career opportunities.

Studying Abroad 59

Discussion Us Groups

- Talk about the questions below.
- Use the **Conversation Strategies** at the bottom of the page.

1 Why do people study abroad?
▶ Explain your ideas.

2 Do you want to study overseas?
▶ Why? Why not? Explain your reasons.

3 What are the advantages of studying abroad?
▶ How many can you think of?

4 What are the disadvantages of studying abroad?
▶ Do the advantages outweigh the disadvantages?

5 Is overseas study only for rich students?
▶ Why? Why not? Support your opinion.

6 If you graduated from a foreign university, would you come back to Korea?
▶ Why? Why not? Support your opinion.

7 Is it necessary to go abroad to study English?
▶ Why? Why not? Support your opinion.

8 What do you think of English Villages?
▶ Have you ever been to one?
▶ What are the advantages and disadvantages?

9 'Overseas study will help you get a good job in Korea.'
▶ Do you agree with this statement?
▶ Why? Why not? Explain your opinion.

10 'Overseas study will change your life.'
▶ Do you agree with this statement?
▶ Why? Why not? Support your opinion.

Conversation Strategies.

Generalizing:		Expressing doubts:	
Generally, Usually, As a rule, On the whole, All things considered,	studying abroad is the experience of a lifetime.	Yes, but on the other hand, Yes, but don't forget, You have a point, but … Possibly, but … That may be so, but …	there can be disadvantages.

Dialogue

- Listen to Track 40 on the CD-Rom.
- Read the dialogue with your partner.
- Perform the dialogue together.
- Change roles. Perform the dialogue again.

(Ji-hye is standing at a bus stop. Mrs. Brown is driving her car.)

Mrs. Brown	Hello, Ji-hye. Can I give you a lift?
Ji-hye	Yes, if that's OK with you. I'm going to my skating class.
Mrs. Brown	Of course. It's on my way.
Ji-hye	Thanks, Mrs. Brown. That's very kind of you.
Mrs. Brown	Don't mention it, Ji-hye. How are things these days?
Ji-hye	Not bad. I like living here.
Mrs. Brown	No plans to go back to Korea?
Ji-hye	I'm thinking of going there later on, to study Korean.
Mrs. Brown	Can't your parents teach you?
Ji-hye	Not really. It's completely different learning in the actual country.
Mrs. Brown	I suppose it's hard to find people to talk with here.
Ji-hye	It's not just that. In Korea you have to use the language in order to survive.
Mrs. Brown	Whereas here …
Ji-hye	You've got it. I don't need to speak Korean here, so I don't study very hard.
Mrs. Brown	Oh well, it sounds like a good plan. We'll miss you.
Ji-hye	Don't worry, Mrs. Brown. I'm not leaving yet. Ah, here's the school. Thanks for the lift!

Key Words and Expressions

"Can I give you a lift?"
"Shall I give you a ride in my car?"

"No plans to "…?
"Don't you have any plans to …?"

"You've got it."
"That's correct." "You've hit the nail on the head."

Dialogue Quiz

1. Is Mrs. Brown going skating?
2. Is Ji-hye satisfied with her situation?
3. Why is she thinking of going to Korea?
4. Why can't she learn Korean from her parents?
5. Will she go to Korea soon?
6. Will she go with Seung-min?

Debate Corner Groups

1. In your group, choose one of the motions below.

> 1. Overseas study is only for rich people.
> 2. Studying abroad is the experience of a lifetime.
> 3. It is not necessary to go abroad to get a good education.
> 4. People who study abroad are helping the future of Korea.

2. Choose one pair (Pro) to agree with your motion, one pair (Con) to disagree, and (if there are 5 people in your group) one person to be the Timekeeper.

Pro/Con Pair, Speaker 1:
▶ These phrases will help you present your arguments.

First of all …	The main thing is …	Furthermore …
To begin with …	The most important thing is …	What's more, …
For a start …	Most importantly …	I might add that …
Next, …	We have to consider that	Not to mention that …
In addition, …	On the one hand …	Plus the fact that …
Finally, …	On the other hand …	Not only that, but …

Pro/Con Pair, Speaker 2
▶ These phrases will help you to reject the other team's arguments.

I disagree.	That isn't the point.	You are mistaken.
I disagree entirely.	That's debatable.	I'm not sure about that.
On the contrary.	That's very unlikely.	I don't know about that.
Definitely not!	That isn't strictly true.	That depends …
That's ridiculous!	I'm afraid you're wrong.	That's a good point, but …
You can't be serious!	I'm afraid I can't agree.	You have a point, but …

Timekeeper:
▶ These phrases will help you control the debate.

Today's motion is …	Speaking for the motion is ….
You have two minutes to speak.	Speaking against the motion is ….
Your time is up.	The next speaker is …
Next speaker please.	The motion has been accepted.
Your conclusions please.	The motion has been rejected.

Let's Debate!

1. **Pro Pair:** Write three reasons for agreeing with the motion, plus your conclusion
2. **Con Pair:** Write three reasons for disagreeing with the motion, plus your conclusion.
3. **Timekeeper:** Look at pages 62 and 64 and think of how to start and end the debate.

First of all, ...
_____
_____
_____

Next, ...
_____
_____
_____

Furthermore, ...
_____
_____
_____

In conclusion, ...
_____
_____
_____

There is a brief sample debate on the next page.

Let's Begin! Us Groups

Timekeeper:

1. Start the debate (see pages 62 and 64).
2. Ask the first Pro speaker to state the 'Pro' arguments.
   Tell him/her that he/she has 1 (or 2) minute(s).
3. Ask the first Con speaker to state the 'Con' arguments.
   Tell him/her that he/she has 1 (or 2) minute(s).
4. Ask the second Pro student to speak and give his/her conclusions.
   Tell him/her that he/she has 1 (or 2) minute(s).
5. Ask the second Con student to speak and give his/her conclusions.
   Tell him/her that he/she has 1 (or 2) minute(s).
6. End the debate (see pages 62 and 64). Either you can decide which team had the best arguments, or you can ask another group to decide.

Debate Sample **Groups**

- Here is a debate sample to give you some ideas.
- The motion is 'Studying abroad is the experience of a lifetime.'
- Can you find the phrases from pages 55 and 62?

Timekeeper: Today's debate is on the motion 'Studying abroad is the experience of a lifetime.' Speaker 1 for the Pro Team, please give your arguments in favor of the motion. You have one minute.

Pro Speaker 1: I am in favor of the motion, for three reasons. To begin with, studying abroad gives us the opportunity to visit famous places such as museums and galleries. We can visit the houses of important historical people and learn about the art of different countries. Secondly, we can meet international students from many different countries and learn about their cultures. Most importantly, we can broaden our minds and our global outlook by studying in an international learning situation.

Timekeeper: Thank you. Now I call upon Speaker 1 for the Con Team. Please give your rebuttal of Pro Speaker 1's arguments. You have one minute.

Con Speaker 1: I disagree entirely with Pro Speaker 1. I am afraid he is mistaken. For a start, there are many problems with studying abroad. Many students experience culture shock and homesickness. Furthermore, they often have great difficulty in understanding the lectures. Studying in an unfamiliar country and culture can be an unsettling experience and can make students give up studying. So I can't agree with the motion. The experience of a lifetime might turn out to be a bad experience.

Timekeeper: Thank you, Con Speaker 1. Now I call upon the audience. You have heard the arguments for and against the motion that studying abroad is the experience of a lifetime. All in favor of the proposition, please raise your hands. All those against the proposition, please raise your hands. I now declare that the motion has been accepted/rejected.

Further Reading: There are more debate links and interesting activities at www.inkbooks.co.kr.

Unit 8 Art and Music

Brainstorming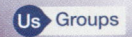

- How many artists can you name?
- How many musicians or composers can you name?
- How many pop stars can you think of?

Task 1 — Groups

20 Questions

Step 1. Student A: Think of a famous artist, musician, composer, or pop star.
Step 2. Other people: Ask questions about the person.

- Is this person a man?
- Is this person a woman?
- Is he/she a movie star?
- Is he/she a pop star?
- Is he/she a musician?
- Is he/she a composer?
- Is he/she a singer?
- Is he/she an artist?

- Is he/she Korean?
- Is he/she American?
- Is he/she from … ?
- Is he/she alive?
- Is/was he/she on TV?
- Did he/she sing …?
- Did he/she wear glasses?
- Did he/she play guitar?

1	2	3	4
5	6	7	8
9	10	11	12
13	14	15	16
17	18	19	20

Step 3. Student A: Only answer 'Yes' or 'No.' Count the questions on the chart.

Task 2

Interview

- Interview your partner. Ask these questions and write the answers in the boxes.

Interviewer	Interviewee
Who is your favorite artist?	
Who is your favorite musician?	
Who is your favorite pop star?	
Who is your favorite singer?	
Whom do you admire most?	
Why do you admire him/her?	
What is he/she famous for?	
Do you want to be like him/her?	
Why? Why not?	

Art as Therapy

- Read this passage together and listen to track 42.
- While you read, match the words and definitions at the bottom of the page.

Art has existed for almost as long as humans and is one of the things that distinguishes us from other species. When we dance, paint a picture, or play a musical instrument, we are being creative. This creative process is very important for personal development. It helps us to concentrate, manage our emotions and increase our confidence.

Through art we think about our place in the universe and express our ideas about life. In addition, artistic hobbies and pastimes are great for reducing stress. Because of this, art therapy, music therapy, and dance therapy have become popular ways of dealing with various sicknesses.

Art therapy improves the physical, mental and emotional health of people of all ages and helps them to explore their problems through pictures. Dance therapy lets people release their feelings through movement, while music therapy helps them to manage stress and improve their social skills through making music with others.

The arts are often neglected in schools, in favor of science and math. But when we look at the work of artists such as Leonardo da Vinci, Michelangelo, and M. C. Escher, along with the recent science of fractals, we find that art and math are closely linked. It has also been shown that students who play musical instruments have significantly improved concentration and memory. Because of this they score higher in standardized tests. Perhaps it is time to revive the arts in education.

Match the words on the left to the definitions on the right.

existed	a type of treatment for a disease or illness
distinguish	able to make new things or ideas
creative	continued to be
therapy	have control of; take care of
release	ignored; dismissed; passed over
manage	let go; free
social skills	methods for relating to other people
neglected	noticeably; in a way that is important
fractals	show a difference; make special
significantly	special figures that have the same structure at every level.

Further Reading: There are more reading passages at www.inkbooks.co.kr

Comprehension Check

1. How are humans different from other species?
2. Why is creativity important?
3. What does art help us to do?
4. How does art therapy help people?
5. How does dance therapy help people?
6. Why is art often ignored in schools?
7. How does playing a musical instrument help us?
8. What is the conclusion of this passage?

Think for Yourself

- [ ] What is art?
- [ ] Is art important in your school?
- [ ] Would you like to paint, dance, or play an instrument?
- [ ] What do you know about M.C. Escher? [Do a Google search.]

Background Information

Did you know?

- [ ] When we hear music, we start to breathe deeply.
- [ ] Music can reduce pain during a visit to the dentist.
- [ ] Background music can reduce stress.
- [ ] Music can reduce heart rates and promote higher body temperatures, helping relaxation.
- [ ] Leonardo da Vinci (1452-1519) was an Italian artist. He also studied mechanics, geometry, mathematics and optics.
- [ ] M. C. Escher (1898 – 1972) created works of art that explored a wide range of mathematical ideas.
- [ ] Johann Sebastian Bach (1685 - 1750) made use of mathematical patterns in his organ works. He often used the Fibonacci series (1, 1, 2, 3, 5, 8, 13 etc.).
- [ ] The ex-president of the USA, Bill Clinton, plays saxophone.
- [ ] Benjamin Franklin (1706 - 1790) played guitar and violin.
- [ ] The parents of Claude Monet (1849 – 1926) thought he would not make a good living if he became an artist.
- [ ] Over 1 million Canadian adults take dance classes.
- [ ] The best engineers and technical designers in the Silicon Valley industry (computer software) are also musicians.

Discussion Groups

- Talk about the questions below.
- Use the **Conversation Strategies** at the bottom of the page.

1 What is art?
  - ▶ How is art different from science?
  - ▶ Explain your ideas.

2 Would you like to be an artist, musician, or dancer?
  - ▶ Why? Why not? Support your opinion.

3 Can you name some artists and composers from earlier centuries?
  - ▶ Why are they still famous after their deaths?
  - ▶ Are there any living artists and musicians who will be famous 100 years later?

4 Should art, music and dance be taught in schools?
  - ▶ Should they be as important as science and math?
  - ▶ Why? Why not? Support your opinion.

5 Have you ever been to an art festival?
  - ▶ Why are there lots of art festivals in Korea these days?
  - ▶ Explain your point of view.

6 Have you ever been to a live concert, a dance performance, or an art exhibition?
  - ▶ What did you think of it (them)?
  - ▶ Explain your feelings about the experience(s).

7 Is pop art (Hallyu, K-pop) really art?
  - ▶ Why? Why not? Support your opinion.

8 What do you think of modern art (video art, etc.)?
  - ▶ Explain your views.

9 Do you believe that art, dance and music can heal people?
  - ▶ Why? Why not? Support your opinion.

Vincent Van Gogh

Conversation Strategies.

Expressing strong opinions:		Mild agreement/disagreement:
I really feel that … I'm convinced that … I'm positive that … I'm absolutely sure that … I'm certain that … Without a doubt,	science and art are both important in our lives.	You could be right. You might have a point. I'm not sure. Do you really think so? I don't know about that. I'm not sure I agree.

Dialogue

- Listen to Track 43 on the CD-Rom.
- Read the dialogue with your partners.
- Perform the dialogue together.
- Change roles. Perform the dialogue again.

Track 43

Key Words and Expressions

"It's not his cup of tea."
"He doesn't like this sort of thing."
"It's not his style."

"You've made your point."
"You have a good point."
"You are right."

(Grandma is sitting at her desk. Ji-hye is watching her.)

Ji-hye	Wow, Grandma Brown, that's fantastic!
Grandma Brown	Thank you, Ji-hye.
Ji-hye	You never told me you were an artist.
Grandma Brown	There are lots of things you don't know about me, Ji-hye.
Ji-hye	That's a beautiful painting. What will you do with it?
Grandma Brown	Maybe I'll put it in my room, along with all the others.
Ji-hye	I'd love to take a look some time, if that's OK.
Grandma Brown	Of course. Ah, here's Kevin.
Kevin	Hi, Ji-hye. Hello, grandma. What's new?
Ji-hye	Look at this, Kevin. Grandma Brown's just painted it!
Kevin	Hmm. It's OK, I suppose.
Grandma Brown	Don't worry, Ji-hye. It's not his cup of tea.
Ji-hye	Why not, Kevin?
Kevin	Sorry, but I prefer science and math. I'm not the 'arty' type.
Grandma Brown	Who's your favorite scientist, Kevin?
Ji-hye	It's Albert Einstein, isn't it?
Grandma Brown	Well, Kevin. Einstein loved art and music. He said 'I often think in music. I see my life in terms of music.'
Kevin	OK, grandma. You've made your point.
Ji-hye	Let's go and look at Grandma Brown's paintings.

Dialogue Quiz

1. What is Grandma Brown doing at the beginning of the dialogue?
2. Why doesn't Kevin think the painting is fantastic?
3. Is Ji-hye an 'arty' type?
4. Who is Kevin's favorite scientist?
5. Why did Grandma Brown say that Einstein loved music?
6. What will they all do next?

Art and Music 69

Debate Corner

1. In your group (4 or 5 people), choose one of the motions below.

> 1. Art is the greatest expression of humanity.
> 2. Money is all that matters. Art is just entertainment.
> 3. Art and music are unnecessary in schools.
> 4. Art and music help us physically and mentally.

2. Choose one pair (Pro) to agree with your motion, one pair (Con) to disagree with it, and (if there are 5 people in your group) one person to be the Timekeeper/Chairperson.

Pro/Con Pair, Student 1:
▶ These phrases will help you present your arguments.

What I'm saying is	Let me put it another way.	For this reason …
I'm saying that …	Don't misunderstand me.	Owing to this, …
The point is that …	What I'm trying to say is …	This is why …
I'm talking about …	That's not what I said.	Therefore,
What I mean is …	That's not what I meant.	As a result,
Don't get me wrong.	Let's get it straight.	Consequently,

Pro/Con Pair, Student 2
▶ These phrases will help you to reject the other team's arguments.

What do you mean?	What are you trying to say?	That may be so, but …
How do you mean?	Can you explain why …?	That may be true, but …
In what way?	Why do you think that?	You may be right, but …
Why do you say that?	You can't mean that!	Possibly, but …
Why is that?	Do you really think that?	What bothers me is …
Come off it!	That's ridiculous!	What I don't like is …

Timekeeper/Chairperson:
These phrases will help you control the debate. In addition, check out the debate sample on page 72.

Today's motion is …	Speaking for the motion is ….
You have two minutes to speak.	Speaking against the motion is ….
Your time is up.	The next speaker is …
Next speaker please.	The motion has been accepted.
Your conclusions please.	The motion has been rejected.

Let's Debate! Us Groups

1. **Pro Pair:** Write three reasons for agreeing with the motion, plus your conclusion
2. **Con Pair:** Write three reasons for disagreeing with the motion, plus your conclusion.
3. **Timekeeper/Chairperson:** Look at pages 70 and 72. Think of how you will run the debate.

First of all, ...

_____

_____

_____

Next, ...

_____

_____

_____

Furthermore, ...

_____

_____

_____

In conclusion, ...

_____

_____

_____

Argument samples

Here are two argument samples to give you some ideas. They are based on motion #2: Money is all that matters. Art is just entertainment.

Pro Speaker 1: To begin with, I'm absolutely certain that the world is becoming money-crazy. Everything we see on TV and in magazines tells us that money equals happiness. On the contrary, we have deep inner feelings which can only be expressed through art and music. What I'm saying is we're losing the joy of dancing, painting, singing and playing. This joy can't be bought with money. Let me put it another way. Even if you become rich, life will have no meaning if you can't appreciate the beauty of art. Your life will be empty and meaningless.

Con Speaker 1: That may be so, but I don't' have much time for things like concerts, operas, art galleries and museums. Don't misunderstand me. They're OK for old people, but they're a waste of time for me. The point is I need to study for my exams so I can go to a good university and get a good job. Artists talk about the meaning of life, but for me that means earning a good wage and taking care of my future family. Maybe I'll learn how to play piano when I'm rich, but before that, there's no time to spare.

Let's Debate! Us Groups

- Listen to the chairperson's remarks on Track 46 on the CD-Rom.
- This sample shows how to run the debate smoothly.
- When you have finished listening, begin your debate.
- The chairperson should use the phrases below.

Timekeeper/Chairperson: Good afternoon ladies and gentlemen.

My name is _____ and I am the chairperson and timekeeper for today's debate.

The motion is _____.

Speaking for the motion are _____ and _____.
Speaking against the motion are _____ and _____.

Now I'd like to call upon the first Pro speaker, _____, to start the debate.
    Speaker Pro 1 gives his/her three reasons.

Thank you, now I'd like to call upon the first Con speaker, _____.
    Speaker Con 1 gives his/her three reasons.

Now we've had our main speeches, are there any questions from the floor?.
    Audience members can ask questions.
    These are usually answered by Speakers Pro 2 and Con 2 in their speeches.

Thank you for your questions. Now we will hear the summary speeches.

I'd like to call upon the second Pro speaker, _____ to sum up.
    Speaker Pro 2 answers the questions, then gives his/her speech and conclusion.

Thank you. Now for the second Con speaker, _____. Please sum up.
    Speaker Con 2 answers the questions, then gives his/her speech and conclusion.

Now we have heard everything, it is time to put the motion to a vote. All those in favor of the motion please raise your hands. All those against the motion, please raise your hands. Thank you. I declare that the motion has been passed/rejected.

Unit 9 Internet Shopping

Brainstorming

- What do you think of Internet Shopping?
- What do other people think?
- Let's perform an Online Shopping survey to find out.

Task 1

Online Shopping Survey

1. Each person - Choose one of the boxes below.
2. Ask the questions in the box to people in other groups.
3. Summarize the answers at the bottom of the page.

A. Online Shopping Sites

Q1. How often do you visit online shopping sites?
Q2. What is your favorite site?
Q3. Do you check the prices on other sites?
Q4. Have you ever used an auction site (ebay, eBid, Webstore, ePier, etc.)?

B. Shopping experience

Q1. Did the item that you bought arrive on time?
Q2. Were you satisfied with it when it arrived?
Q3. Was it as advertised (too big/small, wrong color)?
Q4. Did you experience any problems (damaged, wrong type)?

C. Digital goods

Q1. What sort of digital goods have you bought (software, MP3 files, etc.)?
Q2. Did you use a credit card, PayPal, or online bank transfer?
Q3. Were the digital items downloaded successfully?
Q4. Did they contain any viruses, spyware, or malware?

D. Shareware and freeware

Q1. What sort of shareware or freeware did you choose?
Q2. Did it download successfully?
Q3. Was the freeware really free or did it have a trial period?
Q4. Did you buy the full version later on?

Task 2

Data Collection

- Summarize the answers to each question here. Then report back to your group.

The people I asked said that:

Qu. 1. _____
Qu. 2. _____
Qu. 3. _____
Qu. 4. _____

Computer Scams

Track 47

• Read this passage together and listen to Track 47.
• While you read, match the words and definitions at the bottom of the page.

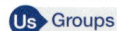

Us Groups

https://www.microsoft.com/ko-kr/

Microsoft 공식 홈페이지

Beware of scams - Protect your computer!

Did you know that your computer can be attacked by scams? Protect your computer now. If you don't, you might find some expensive payments on your next credit card bill!

Here are some ways to protect your computer.

1. Use a firewall and anti-virus software. These prevent viruses and malicious software (malware) from sending secret information from your computer.
   - Download and install the latest security patches for all your software.
   - Use an auto-update function if possible.

2. Don't reply to unsolicited emails. Spam messages can install malware on your computer.
   - Think before you click.
   - Be suspicious of emails promising easy money.
   - Be skeptical of offers that are too good to be true. They usually are!
   - Don't disclose personal information if you can help it.
   - Never reply to an email asking for confidential details such as passwords.

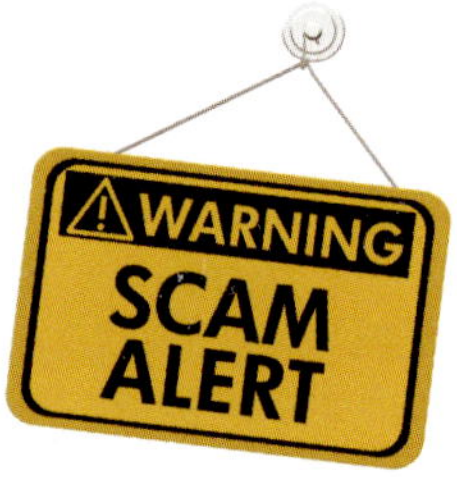

Match the words on the left to the definitions on the right.

scam •	• a dishonest scheme or trick
firewall •	• a security block on a computer
malicious •	• an upgrade; a bug fix; a new update
patch •	• doubtful; unbelieving
unsolicited •	• evil; bad; nasty; wicked
skeptical •	• make known; reveal; uncover
disclose •	• not looked for; not asked for
confidential •	• strictly private; secret

Further Reading: There are more reading passages at www.inkbooks.co.kr

Comprehension Check

1. According to the passage, what are three ways to protect your computer?
2. What can happen if you don't protect your computer?
3. How do firewalls and anti-virus software help you?
4. Why do you need security patches?
5. Why is spam mail dangerous?
6. Can you find a word similar in meaning to 'skeptical' in the passage?
7. Can you find a word opposite in meaning to 'install' in the passage?
8. You should never reply to unsolicited emails. ☐ True ☐ False

Think for Yourself

☐ Where would you expect to see this message?
☐ Have you ever opened unsolicited emails?
☐ Why do you think people make viruses and malware?

Background Information

Did you know?

☐ Online shopping sales grew to $370 billion in 2016, up from $231 billion in 2012.

☐ 72% percent of young people check prices online before going to a store.

☐ The greatest category of people using the Internet are adults 50 years old and above.

☐ There are 195.3 million Internet users in the U.S.

☐ On peak days, Amazon sells 320 items per second.

☐ 75% of men and women in the US have shopped online. People who have been using the Internet for some time do many things online, from buying goods, booking trips, and reserving movie tickets, to banking online.

☐ A few years ago, only young, rich people used to shop on the Internet. Now, older Americans are shopping online, along with people who don't have a university education.

☐ In 2016, there were 41 million Internet users in Korea. This was 84% of the population.

☐ 84.8% of Koreans browse the Internet on their mobile phones.

Internet Shopping 75

Discussion Groups

- Talk about the questions below.
- Use the **Conversation Strategies** at the bottom of the page.

1 Do you do Internet shopping?
   - How often do you shop online?
   - What do you buy?
   - Where do you buy it from?

2 What are some advantages of Internet shopping?
   - Explain your ideas and your experiences.

3 What are some disadvantages of Internet shopping?
   - Explain your ideas and your experiences.

4 Are people are addicted to online shopping these days?
   - Why? Why not? Support your opinion.

5 Does Internet shopping encourage people to get into debt?
   - Why? Why not? Explain your reasons.

6 Have you ever had spyware, malware, a worm, or a virus on your computer?
   - What did you do about it?

7 What is phishing?
   - Have you had an experience of phishing?
   - How can you recognize a phishing email?

8 What is a hacker? What do hackers do?
   - Why do people phish and hack?

9 How can Internet criminals be caught and punished?
   - Explain your ideas.

Conversation Strategies.

Expressing your opinion: Disagreeing politely:

Frankly speaking, …	You could be right, but …	That may be so, but …
To tell the truth, …	You have a point, but …	We must remember that …
In my opinion …	On the other hand …	I can't agree with you.
You're absolutely right!	I know what you mean, but …	I'm afraid I don't agree.
I agree up to a point.	Please bear in mind that …	I think you're mistaken.

Dialogue

- Listen to Track 48 on the CD-Rom.
- Read the dialogue with your partner.
- Perform the dialogue together.
- Change roles. Perform the dialogue again.

Key Words and Expressions

shopping site
an Internet site that sells goods online

take a chance
risk; take a risk

"Let's grab a coffee."
"Let's go and have a cup of coffee."

Grandma Brown	Hello, Kevin. What's new?
Kevin	Hello, grandma. I've found this great shopping site online.
Grandma Brown	Hmm. Looks interesting. What are you looking for?
Kevin	I'm buying flowers for mum and dad's wedding anniversary.
Grandma Brown	Can't you get them downtown, at the florist?
Kevin	Of course, but they're cheaper online, and they deliver the flowers for me. The Internet saves me a lot of time.
Grandma Brown	Aren't you afraid of putting your credit card details on the Internet?
Kevin	I know what you mean, grandma, but this site is safe. Don't worry.
Grandma Brown	I'd rather not take the chance. It's much too dangerous.
Kevin	Come on, grandma. What could go wrong?
Grandma Brown	Quite a few things, Kevin. Viruses, Internet worms, Spyware, you name it. Check your credit card statement, and make sure you haven't paid for lots of things you didn't buy.
Kevin	You've made your point, grandma. Let's grab a coffee.
Grandma Brown	Right. That's one thing we can't do online – drink coffee!

Dialogue Quiz

1. Why isn't Kevin buying flowers downtown?
2. Is Kevin afraid of putting his credit card details online?
3. What are two advantages of online shopping, according to this passage?
4. What does Grandma Brown think of online shopping?
5. What are three disadvantages of Internet shopping, according to this passage?
6. How will Kevin know if his Internet Identity has been stolen?

Let's Make a Role-play!

- **Situation 1:** A customer is calling an online company to complain. The goods he/she ordered haven't arrived yet.
- **Situation 2:** A customer is calling an online company to complain. The goods that arrived are not what he/she ordered.

1. Choose your role.
2. Read your role-card and the phrases.
3. Think about what you will say in the role-play.
4. Write your ideas on the next page.

Customer

Here are some ideas:

1. Ring the company.
2. Tell the assistant the order number.
3. Explain what you ordered.
4. Explain when you ordered the goods.
5. Explain the problem.
6. Ask for a refund.

Here are some phrases you can use.

- Hello. Is that the …. company?
- I want to make a complaint.
- Order number …
- I sent an email, but nothing happened.
- Why wasn't my email answered?
- I ordered some ………
- That was three weeks ago.
- They haven't arrived yet.
- It has arrived, but it's the wrong color.
- They have arrived, but they're too big/small.
- They are not what I ordered.
- This isn't good enough.
- I expect better service.
- I would like a refund.
- I want my money back.
- No, I don't want to wait for a replacement.
- That would take too long.
- Are you sure it will be OK this time?
- Please give me a discount.
- This has caused me lots of trouble.
- I needed the items last week.
- Thank you. Goodbye.

Customer service assistant

Here are some ideas:

1. Greet the customer.
2. Ask him/her what the problem is.
3. Apologize for the delay/problem.
4. Say you will try to sort it out.
5. Try to make the customer satisfied.
6. Thank the customer.

Here are some useful phrases:

- Good morning/afternoon/evening.
- Can I help you?
- What is your order number?
- When did you send the email?
- I will check with the department.
- I apologize for the inconvenience.
- I'm sorry the goods haven't arrived.
- I will try to find out what has happened.
- I can't give you a refund yet.
- I will get back to you with the answer.
- Could you send the goods back to us?
- We will send you the correct goods.
- I can't give you a discount.
- Yes, I understand your problem.
- This is company policy.
- There is nothing I can do.
- Thank you for shopping with us.

Role-play Storyboard

- With your partner, make a storyboard for your role-play.
- Perform your role-play together.
- Now perform it to another group.

Time to Reflect!

- Fill in this self-assessment and think about your contribution to the role-play.
- Then add your comments. How was your role-play? Did you do your best?

5 = Fantastic, 4 = Pretty good, 3 = OK, 2 = Not too good, 1 = I could do much better

Role-play self-assessment		5	4	3	2	1
1	I contributed to choosing the title.					
2	I contributed to making the plot (story).					
3	I contributed by drawing the pictures.					
4	I contributed by writing the words.					
5	I rehearsed the role-play with my partner.					
6	We performed the role-play to another pair.					
7	Our drama took a reasonable amount of time.					
8	Our drama was interesting.					
9	I used expressive body language.					
10	I was confident and cheerful.					
	Total = _____ / 50					

My comments:

Review

- Now review what you have done in this Unit and prepare for the next Unit.

Review
Browse the website for Unit 9.

Preview
Browse the website for Unit 10.

Prepare
Look at the activities in Unit 10.

Unit 10 Traffic

Brainstorming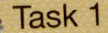

- How do you get to school each day?
- Do you use public transport?
- Do you walk? Do you cycle?

Task 1

Traffic Word Search
How many traffic words can you find in this Word Search?

```
            L N L S U
          Q E E G Z V B E
        N K S E I     F N R
      W J L T H S       L P J
    S L N A R W C         B C X
    U V U W O G I         S M K T S U O
    O B Z L E D N F O O T B R I D G E L V X
    C W M Y D Y I F G N I S S O R C M R E K C
    Q F A C G I T R A F F I C L I G H T O R L F
    Y I Y A W S S E R P X E T N E M E V A P B Q
    H Z J R S A F E T Y B E L T H G I L D A E H
    M H F P C I N T E R S E C T I O N Y E S K B
    F C N A I R T S E D E P K K L O E V X S D
        C R S E                 U M B I
            K L                     Q W
```

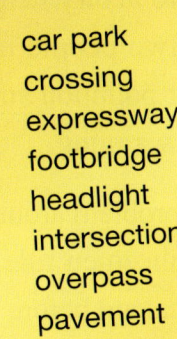

car park   pedestrian
crossing   road
expressway   safety belt
footbridge   sidewalk
headlight   steering wheel
intersection   subway
overpass   traffic light
pavement   traffic sign

*The solution is in the Answer Key, at the back of book.

Task 2

Traffic Rules:
Can you think of some Traffic Rules? Discuss them together.
Write your rules in this Safety First! sign:

Safety First!

1. Car drivers should _____
2. Car drivers should _____
3. Car drivers should not _____
4. Car drivers should not _____
5. Bus drivers should _____
6. Bus drivers should not _____
7. People who walk should _____
8. People who walk should not _____

Traffic 81

Traffic Blues

- Read this passage together and listen to Track 49.
- While you read, match the words and definitions at the bottom of the page.

Chris Warham / Shutterstock.com

Traffic is a fact of life these days. Everywhere we go, we see cars, buses, trucks and taxis. On special holidays like Chuseok and the Lunar New Year, the expressways are bumper-to-bumper with cars and buses. But it hasn't always been like this. In 1955 there were only 6,435 cars in Seoul. By 1970 there were 127,000 cars in Korea and by 2015, this number had risen to 21 million.

In the 1980s, cars were luxury items. Now, at least 1 million new cars are sold every year, and there is one car for every two people in Korea. So it is not surprising that roads are overcrowded and traffic is producing air pollution and noise pollution. In addition, the exhaust gases from vehicles are contributing to global warming.

Traffic has become a problem around the world. It is often quicker to walk or to ride a bike in modern cities. In fact, 500 policemen ride bikes in London and paramedics often cycle to the scene of an accident to give medical aid before the ambulance arrives.

Many cities have banned cars from city centers and are encouraging people to use public transport. Furthermore, self-driving robot cars could make traffic run smoother in the near future. Who knows? Perhaps driving to work will become a thing of the past. We will just press a button and the car will do the rest!

Match the words on the left to the definitions on the right.

fact of life	a person who is trained to give emergency medical care
bumper-to-bumper	barred; forbidden; excluded; prohibited
luxury item	finished; forgotten; no longer in existence
global warming	normal; usual; accepted
paramedic	the heating of the world as a result of pollution
banned	traffic jam; unable to move
a thing of the past	very expensive

Further Reading: There are more reading passages at www.inkbooks.co.kr

Comprehension Check

1. Why is traffic a fact of life?
2. Are the expressways always overcrowded?
3. When were cars luxury items?
4. How many cars were there in Korea in 2015?
5. What are the disadvantages of cars?
6. Why do policemen and paramedics ride bikes in London?
7. What are cities doing about the traffic problem?
8. What are the traffic prospects for the future?

Think for Yourself

- [ ] Is there a lot of traffic near your home?
- [ ] Has the amount of traffic changed in the last 5 years?
- [ ] Have you ever seen a traffic accident?
- [ ] Have you seen cars going through red lights?

Background Information

Did you know?

- [ ] Karl Benz invented the modern car in 1879.
- [ ] There were 256 million motor vehicles in the USA in 2013.
- [ ] There are 3.9 million miles of roads in the USA. If they were put end-to-end, they would circle the earth 157 times.
- [ ] Roads and parking lots in the USA cover 61,000 square miles. That's almost twice the area of South Korea.
- [ ] Every year 50 million cars are added to the world's roads.
- [ ] Car making is the biggest manufacturing industry in the world.
- [ ] In Los Angeles there are more cars than people.
- [ ] Cars kill two people every minute.
- [ ] In 1960, John F Kennedy said that cars were the greatest health problem in the USA.
- [ ] 70% of road deaths happen in developing countries.
- [ ] 65% of road deaths are pedestrians.
- [ ] Road accidents are the 2nd biggest cause of death for men aged between 15 and 44.

Discussion Us Groups

- Talk about the questions below.
- Use the **Conversation Strategies** at the bottom of the page.

1 What are the advantages of private cars?
   ▶ Explain your ideas.

2 What are the disadvantages of private cars?
   ▶ Support your opinions.

3 Are there too many cars on the roads?
   ▶ What can be done about this?

4 Have you ever been in a car accident?
   ▶ YES: Tell everyone about it.
   ▶ NO: Have you seen a car accident?

5 Are women better drivers than men?
   ▶ Explain your opinion.

6 How can the number of traffic jams be reduced?
   ▶ Explain your ideas.

7 Do you use public transport (buses, subway trains, etc.)?
   ▶ How can public transport be improved?

8 What do you think of 'car pooling' (the sharing of cars)?
   ▶ Support your opinion.

9 What will the transport of the future look like?
   ▶ Explain your ideas.

10 Is it OK to build new roads on farming land?
   ▶ What do you think?

Conversation Strategies

Expressing an opinion:

I think …
I suppose …
I'm pretty sure that …
I'm fairly certain that …
I'm convinced that …
I'm sure that …
It seems to me that …

→ there are too many cars on the roads.

Agreement:

Me too!
So do I.
That's just what I think.
That's what I was going to say.
You're absolutely right!
Tell me about it!
You're not kidding!

Dialogue Us Groups

- Listen to Track 50 on the CD-Rom.
- Read the dialogue with your partner.
- Perform the dialogue together.
- Change roles. Perform the dialogue again.

Track 50

(Kevin and Sung-min are walking to the local Baseball Game.)

Sung-min	Come on, Kevin. We're nearly there.
Kevin	You sure walk fast, Sung-min. I can't keep up with you.
Sung-min	You should get more exercise.
Kevin	You mean ride my bike to school?
Sung-min	That's right. Instead of getting a lift from your mum.
Kevin	Anyway, it doesn't matter now. There's the stadium.
Sung-min	And here's the crossing.
Kevin	There's nothing coming, let's cross.
Sung-min	But, Kevin. The light's still on red.
Kevin	Don't worry. Everybody does it.
Sung-min	What if you have an accident?
Kevin	It's quite safe. Just look both ways.
Sung-min	I'd rather wait for the light to change.
Kevin	If you say so.

(The crossing light changes to green.)

Kevin	There! We can cross now.
Sung-min	Better safe than sorry.

Key Words and Expressions

keep up with
match;
walk at the same speed

"The light's on red."
"The red crossing light is showing."

"Look both ways."
"Look left and right before you cross."

"If you say so."
"If that's what you want, then we'll do it."

"Better safe than sorry."
"It's better to be careful, rather than take risks." (proverb)

Dialogue Quiz

1. Why can't Kevin keep up with Sung-min?
2. How can Kevin get more exercise?
3. Why does Kevin think it's OK to cross on the red light?
4. Does Sung-min agree?
5. What do you think 'Better safe than sorry' means in the situation?

Debate Corner

1. In your group (4 or 5 people), choose one of the motions below.

   1. Private cars cause pollution and global warming.
   2. Private cars should be banned in cities.
   3. All vehicles should use electric or solar energy.
   4. Public transport should be free.

2. Choose one pair (Pro) to agree with your motion, one pair (Con) to disagree with it, and (if there are 5 people in your group) one person to be the Timekeeper or Chairperson.

Pro/Con Speaker 1:
▶ These phrases will help you present your arguments strongly:

In my opinion,	I'm sure that …	Clearly, …
In my view,	I'm certain that …	Obviously, …
I strongly believe that	I'm pretty sure that …	There's no doubt that …
I definitely think that	According to statistics,	Whithout doubt, …
Well, if you ask me, …	Actually, …	Undoubtedly, …
Well, I think …	In fact, …	Surely, …

Pro/Con Speaker 2
▶ These phrases will help you to make your conclusions:

Generally, …	To put it simply,	To summarize, …
As a rule, …	So, in short, …	To make a long story short, …
Typically,	All in all, …	To put it in a few words, …
By and large,	In the end, …	In a nutshell, …
On average,	To conclude, …	In brief, …
Generally speaking,	To sum up, …	To be brief, …

Timekeeper/Chairperson:
▶ These phrases will help you control the debate.

Today's motion is …	Speaking for the motion is ….
You have two minutes to speak.	Speaking against the motion is ….
Your time is up.	The next speaker is …
Next speaker please.	The motion has been accepted.
Your conclusions please.	The motion has been rejected.

Let's Prepare! Us Groups

- **Pro Pair/Con Pair:** Look at pages 62, 70 and 86 for debate language and phrases. Then write three reasons for agreeing / disagreeing with the motion, plus your conclusion.
- There are some sample arguments on the next page.
- **Timekeeper/Chairperson:** Look at pages 72 and 86 for ideas and phrases.

First of all, ...

Next, ...

Furthermore, ...

In conclusion, ...

Let's Begin! Us Groups

- **Timekeeper/Chairperson:** Start the debate.
- Use the debate sample on page 72 and the phrases on page 86.
- Here is a checklist to help you.

1	Introduce yourself.	✔
2	State the motion.	
3	Introduce the speakers.	
4	Pro Speaker 1	
5	Con Speaker 1	
6	Questions from the floor	
7	Pro Speaker 2: Summary/Conclusion	
8	Con Speaker 2: Summary/Conclusion	
9	Vote	
10	Final remarks	

Bikeworldtravel / Shutterstock.com

Argument Samples Groups

- Here are two argument samples to give you some ideas (tracks 51 and 52).
- They are about motion #2: 'Private cars should be banned in cities.'
- Can you find phrases from page 86 in these samples?

Pro Speaker 1: In my opinion, the use of private cars in cities must be stopped, for the following reasons. To start with, they are generally causing long traffic jams and blocking public transport. In addition, I strongly believe that they are contributing to global warming. Without doubt, the government should ban cars in cities and make everyone use buses or subway trains. This would make the cities cleaner and people much healthier, especially if they use bicycles or walk.

Con Speaker 1: Well, if you ask me, I just can't imagine not driving in the city. To put it simply, it's so convenient. I don't have to wait for public transport and I can put my shopping in the car, instead of carrying it on the bus. By and large, I can go where I want, when I want, and I don't have to worry about the weather. Generally speaking, I don't like to use public transport. It's such a bother having to change buses or subways. Anyway, I believe it is my right to drive in the city.

Car Park Puzzle

- This car park is very blocked! Can you get the red car to drive out at the EXIT?
- Vehicles can only go forwards or backwards. They cannot turn.
- How many vehicles do you need to move?

*The answer is in the Answer Key at the back of the book.

Unit 11 Culture Shock

Brainstorming *Me*

- What is special about Korean culture?
- Can you explain Korean culture to a foreigner?

Task *Us ▸ Groups*

Culture Board Game
- Play this game together. The rules are at the bottom of the page.

🎲	Korean Folk Village	Samgyetang	Hangeul
Seoraksan Mountain	⚀ What? ⚁ Who?		Chuseok
Bibimbap	⚂ Why? ⚃ Where?		Bulguksa Temple
Mask Dance	⚄ When? ⚅ How?		Kimchi
King Sejong			Gyeongbokgung Palace
Insa-dong	Hanbok	Doenjang	Danpung

1. You need 2 DICE.  Begin in the TOP LEFT Square.
2. **Student A:** Roll ONE die. Move around the board (clockwise).
3. Roll the other die. 1 = What? 2 = Who? 3 = Why? 4 = Where? 5 = When? 6 = How?
4. **Everybody:** Make a question for Student A.
   For example, if Student A has 'Kimchi' and 'How?' you can ask 'How do you make Kimchi?'
5. **Student A:** Answer the question.
6. **Student B:** Roll ONE die. Move around the board (clockwise). Roll the other die …………

Getting to Know You

- Read this passage together and listen to Track 53.
- While you read, match the words and definitions at the bottom of the page.

In our day-to-day lives we take many things for granted, including our culture—the beliefs, customs, arts and way of thinking of people in our society. In fact we usually don't think about it until we go abroad. At that time, we often experience 'culture shock.' We don't know the language, we don't know how to behave and we don't understand the customs. Every day, we meet new ways of thinking and doing things. This can cause severe stress and even depression, until we start to understand the new culture.

What sort of culture shock do foreigners experience when they come to Korea? What do they find unfamiliar? Here are some things that visitors to Korea typically need to know if they are not to feel like a fish out of water.

Newcomers to Korea should:

1. Learn how to bow instead of shaking hands.
2. Never write someone's name in red.
3. Give and receive things with both hands.
4. Never fold their arms in front of older people.
5. Take their shoes off when entering a house or a restaurant.
6. Be on their best behavior as ambassadors for their country.
7. Try to understand if people ask personal questions.
8. When eating out, wait for the oldest person to start eating.
9. Refrain from holding the rice bowl in their hands. This is a Chinese custom.
10. Never blow their nose at the table.

Match the words on the left to the definitions on the right.

take for granted	a state of feeling sad
way of thinking	beliefs; actions; habits
way of life	having a meal at a restaurant
severe	outlook; mindset; frame of mind
depression	queries about age, marriage, money, etc.
fish out of water	representatives
ambassadors	someone who is in an unusual situation
personal questions	to fail to notice something because it is so familiar
eating out	to stop yourself from doing something
refrain	very bad, serious, unpleasant

Further Reading: There are more reading passages at www.inkbooks.co.kr

Comprehension Check

1. What do we normally take for granted?
2. What is culture?
3. When do we experience culture shock?
4. Is it OK in Korea to start eating before elderly people?
5. Why should visitors be on their best behavior?
6. What should they do if people ask personal questions?
7. Do Koreans hold the rice bowl when eating?
8. Can you find another word for 'foreigners' in the passage?

Think for Yourself

- [ ] Why shouldn't visitors to Korea write their names in red?
- [ ] Why should they give and receive things with two hands?
- [ ] Why shouldn't they fold their arms in front of older people?
- [ ] Can you think of any more cultural hints for foreigners?

Background Information

Did you know?

- [ ] In Lebanon, nodding the head means "No".
- [ ] In Saudi Arabia, shaking the head from left to right means "Yes".
- [ ] In Australia, the light switch is turned down to switch on the light. In the United States, the switch is turned up.
- [ ] In Indonesia it is very rude to point with the forefinger. Indonesians point with their thumbs.
- [ ] In Thailand it is considered rude to cross your legs or to point your toes at another person.
- [ ] In Mexico it is rude to stand with your hands on your hips.
- [ ] People in Thailand smile to say Hello, to say Thank you, to apologize, to ask you for something, and to smooth over bad feelings. They even smile when they are happy!
- [ ] Greeks never use credit cards when paying for a meal.
- [ ] In Romania you should never give an even number of flowers (2, 4, 6, …) to a living person.
- [ ] In Russia, you should never leave an empty bottle on the table.

Discussion Groups

- Talk about the questions below.
- Use the **Conversation Strategies** at the bottom of the page.

1 What do you take for granted every day?
   ▶ Talk about your day-to-day lifestyles.

2 Have you ever experienced culture shock?
   ▶ YES: Tell the others about it.
   ▶ NO: What do you know about culture shock?

3 What is special about Korean culture?
   ▶ What do visitors to Korea find unfamiliar or strange?

4 How is Korean culture different from American or European culture?
   ▶ Explain your ideas.

5 Do you think Korean people suffer culture shock when they go abroad?
   ▶ What sort of culture shock do they experience?
   ▶ What do Koreans find strange in other cultures?

6 Do you have any tips for visitors to Korea?
   ▶ Explain your ideas.

7 Is Korean culture disappearing?
   ▶ Is it becoming too Americanized?

8 Is globalization making every culture the same?
   ▶ Explain your opinions.

9 How can people get over culture shock?
   ▶ Make some suggestions.

Conversation Strategies

Stating a common idea:

| Many people think that …
Some people say that …
You must have heard that …
At first it seems that …
It looks as if …
It often seems as if … | Englishmen carry umbrellas all the time. |

Giving a different idea:

| Actually,
In fact,
In reality,
To tell the truth,
Frankly speaking,
The truth of the matter is … | Umbrellas are more popular in Korea and Japan. |

Dialogue

- Listen to Track 54 on the CD-Rom.
- Read the dialogue with your partner.
- Perform the dialogue together.
- Change roles. Perform the dialogue again.

(Seung-min is seated, drawing a picture. Mr. Brown enters the room.)

Seung-min	Hello, Mr. Brown.
Mr. Brown	Hi, Seung-min. What are you doing?
Seung-min	I'm drawing American Indians in front of their tents.
Mr. Brown	Oh, yes. It's very good.
Seung-min	Do you think so? I'm really interested in Indian tribes.
Mr. Brown	You're quite multi-cultural. Aren't you?
Seung-min	I suppose I have to be.
Mr. Brown	What do you mean?
Seung-min	Don't get me wrong. I love living in the USA, but …
Mr. Brown	But what? What's the problem?
Seung-min	Well, it's not easy being from another country.
Mr. Brown	I know what you mean, Seung-min. It must be difficult.
Seung-min	It's not just culture shock. I got over that long ago.
Mr. Brown	Give it time. Things will get better.
Seung-min	I hope so. Sometimes I feel like I'm from another planet.
Mr. Brown	It's not that bad, Seung-min. Cheer up!

Key Words and Expressions

Indian tribes
communities of North American Indians; clans

multicultural
knowing about different cultures

"Don't get me wrong."
"Don't misunderstand me."

"I have to be."
"I have no choice."

"Give it time."
"Have patience."
"Time heals all things."

from another planet
our of place;
strange and unusual

Dialogue Quiz

1. Describe the picture that Seung-min is drawing.
2. Why does Seung-min 'have to be' multi-cultural?
3. Does Seung-min want to go back to Korea?
4. Is Seung-min suffering from culture shock?
5. What is Mr. Brown's advice to Seung-min?
6. What does Seung-min mean by 'another planet'?

Let's Make a Travel Role-play!

- **Situation:** Three friends are planning to go on a trip for two weeks.
- **Task:** You will make a role-play in which the friends make their plans together.
- **Preparation:** 1. Look at the role-play cards on this page.
    2. Choose your role and think about what you will say.
    3. Write your ideas on the next page.

Friend 1 (Visiting Europe)

You have read a lot about Europe and you have seen TV programs about famous cities in Europe. You want to visit Rome, Florence, Paris, London and Prague. You want to visit famous art galleries and museums. You are sure this would be a wonderful holiday. It would be the experience of a lifetime. You and your friends could see the Mona Lisa and the Eiffel Tower. You could also learn about European culture and talk with Europeans.

Friend 2 (Adventure holiday)

You don't want a normal holiday. Everyone visits famous places. That's not exciting at all. You want to do something different. You want to go to Africa and see the animals in a game park. Imagine seeing lions and elephants and giraffes! On the other hand, how about seeing the Mayan Ruins at Cancun, Mexico? There is also a great beach there. You could go snorkeling as well!

Friend 3 (Beach holiday)

You want a relaxing holiday. You don't want to spend all your time going round cities or doing extreme sports like rafting and bungee jumping. You want to take it easy, lie on a beautiful white beach and swim in the sea when you feel like it. You could read your favorite books and go to jazz clubs and discos in the evening. Vacations are times to relax and recover from normal life. There are lots of wonderful places where you could do that. How about Bali, Brazil, Cuba or even Puerto Rico?

Role-play Script

- Make a script for your role-play. You can work on this together.
- Do you think you would experience culture shock on your vacation?
- Rehearse your role-play. Then perform it to another group.
- How about making a video?

Title:

Characters:

Location:

Brain Teasers

- Can you find the solutions to these puzzles?
- The answers are in the Answer Section at the back of the book.

Puzzle 1: There are 6 apples in a basket. Six people each take one apple. However, there is one apple left in the basket. What has happened?

Puzzle 2: A man and his son are in a car crash. The father is dead but the son is taken to hospital. The surgeon says 'I can't operate. This is my son.' How can this be true?

Puzzle 3: I flip a coin 4 times. The first time it comes down heads. The second and third times it comes down heads. What are the chances of it coming down tails next time?

Puzzle 4: A man lives on the 18th floor of a building. He takes the elevator each day to go to work. In the evening, he takes the elevator to the 12th floor. Then he walks up the stairs to reach his apartment. Why does he do this?

Puzzle 5: Three people have a meal in a restaurant. The cost is $30 so they each pay $10. The manager decides to give them a discount of $5. However, the waiter keeps $2 and gives $1 to each person. Each person has now paid $9 and the waiter has $2. But (3 x 9) + 2 = $29. So where is the missing $1?

There are more puzzles and other activities on the website at www.inkbooks.co.kr.

Unit 12 Proverbs

Brainstorming

- What are proverbs?
- How do they help us in life?
- Do you know many Korean proverbs?

Task 1

Proverb Matching
- Match the beginning and ending of these proverbs:

A bird in the hand	in a day.
A friend in need	in one basket.
Actions speak louder	is a friend indeed.
All that glitters	is not gold.
An apple a day	is worth two in the bush.
As you sow,	keeps the doctor away.
Don't put all your eggs	make the most noise.
Empty vessels	so shall you reap.
Rome was not built	than words.
Where there's a will,	there's a way.

Task 2

Proverbs and Meanings
- Write the proverbs above their explanations:

Don't put all your hopes on one thing. Have a backup plan.

Anybody can talk, but it's what you do that counts.

If you really want to do something, you will find a way of doing it.

A real friend is someone who helps you when you are in trouble.

People who don't know much do the most talking.

Hold on to what you have, instead of going after something that looks better.

The answers to Tasks 1 and 2 are in the Answer Section at the back of the book.

The Early Bird

- Read this passage together and listen to Track 55.
- While you read, match the words and definitions at the bottom of the page.

 Groups

Proverbs tell us simple, basic truths that have been passed down by our ancestors. These are often similar in different parts of the world, since human beings face similar problems wherever they are. For example, 'Actions speak louder than words' appears in Africa as: 'A chattering bird builds no nest' and in China as: 'Talk does not cook rice.'

On the other hand, there are also many proverbs that express the unique culture of a country:

- One finger cannot lift a pebble. (Iran)
- When elephants battle, the ants die. (Cambodia)
- Better to be a free bird than a captive King. (Denmark)
- Better bread with water than cake with trouble. (Russia)
- It takes a village to raise a child. (Africa)

In the west, many proverbs come from *The Bible*. In fact, the *Old Testament* contains a whole section called *The Book of Proverbs*. Here is an example: 'A wise son makes his father glad, but a foolish son is a grief to his mother.'

Finally, some proverbs are contradictory, so we have to be careful. When we are thinking of trying something new, for example, we have to choose between: 'Look before you leap,' and 'He who hesitates is lost.' Then again, if we need help, 'Many hands make light work' gives the opposite advice to 'Too many cooks spoil the broth.'

All in all, proverbs give us the wisdom of the ancients in short, simple, easy-to-remember sentences. However, we have to be careful about which proverb we choose!

Match the words on the left to the definitions on the right.

chattering	a small town or community
unique	not free; prisoner
captive	sadness
village	saying opposite things
Old Testament	soup; stew
grief	talking quickly, about nothing special
contradictory	the first part of the Christian bible
hesitate	the only one; single
broth	to pause or wait because of fear

Further Reading: There are more reading passages at www.inkbooks.co.kr

Comprehension Check

1. According to the passage, what do proverbs tell us?
2. Why do similar proverbs turn up in different countries?
3. Can you explain the Danish proverb in the passage?
4. Can you explain the second African proverb in the passage?
5. Can you find another word that means 'ancestors' in the passage?
6. How is 'Look before you leap' different from 'He who hesitates is lost'?
7. How is 'Many hands make light work' different from 'Too many cooks spoil the broth'?

Think for Yourself

- ☐ Do you know any other English proverbs?
- ☐ Make your own one-sentence proverb:

    My proverb : _____.

Background Information

Did you know?

- ☐ The study of proverbs is called paremiology.
- ☐ Aesop's fables have proverbs (or 'morals') at the end.
- ☐ The average number of words in a proverb is 7.
- ☐ Proverbs are anonymous. (They have no author.)
- ☐ Some proverbs use the same letters at the beginning of words: '<u>F</u>orgive and <u>f</u>orget.'
- ☐ Some proverbs repeat the same words: '<u>Nothing</u> ventured, <u>nothing</u> gained.'
- ☐ Some proverbs use rhyme: 'An apple a <u>day</u> keeps the doctor <u>away</u>.' 'When the cat's <u>away</u>, the mice will <u>play</u>.'
- ☐ Some proverbs use repetition and rhyme: '<u>A friend</u> <u>in need</u> is <u>a friend</u> <u>indeed</u>.'
- ☐ The film 'Forrest Gump' uses many proverbs.
- ☐ Some rock bands have used parts of proverbs to make their names. For example: 'Rolling Stones.' Two groups have even called themselves 'The Proverbs.'

Discussion Groups

- Talk about the questions below.
- Use the **Conversation Strategies** at the bottom of the page.

1 Do you know any Korean proverbs?
  ▶ Tell us about them.

2 Do you know any of Aesop's fables?
  ▶ Tell us a fable.
  ▶ What is the lesson of the fable?

3 What is your favorite proverb?
  ▶ Tell us about it.

4 Are ancient proverbs still true in modern life?
  ▶ Why? Why not? Support your opinion.

5 Here are some modern proverbs:
  ▶ You cant recycle wasted time.
  ▶ If you can't stand the heat, get out of the kitchen.
  ▶ If you break it, you buy it.
  ▶ Wake up and smell the coffee.
  ▶ When the going gets tough, the tough get going.
  ▶ If you want your dreams to come true, don't oversleep.
  ▶ Ideas won't work unless you do.
  ▶ A friend walks in when everyone else walks out.
  • What do you think these proverbs mean?

6 T-Shirts often have modern proverbs on them:
  ▶ Out of my mind. Back in five minutes.
  ▶ Time flies like an arrow. Fruit flies like a banana.
  • What words would you put on a T-Shirt?

Conversation Strategies

Giving unusual information:

| Guess what?
Do you know what?
Believe it or not,
You'll never believe it, but …
Are you ready for this? | Slow and steady wins the race. |

Responding:

Really?
Is that so?
You're kidding!
You're joking!
Are you serious?

Dialogue

- Listen to Track 56 on the CD-Rom.
- Read the dialogue with your partner.
- Perform the dialogue together.
- Change roles. Perform the dialogue again.

Key Words and Expressions

"I don't think purple is his color."
"Purple doesn't suit him."
"He doesn't like purple."

"I can't make head or tail of it."
"I can't understand it at all."

cool
fashionable; smart; 'with it'

(Mrs. Brown and Jenny are shopping in a department store.)

Jenny	Hey, mum. How about this jacket?
Mrs. Brown	Hmm. It's nice, but I don't think purple is his color.
Jenny	You're probably right. There's got to be something for dad here.
Mrs. Brown	Let's look in the book department. Your father loves reading.
Jenny	Sure. *(They go down the escalator to the next floor.)*
Mrs. Brown	Ah! Here's something.
Jenny	What's that?
Mrs. Brown	It's a book of Scottish proverbs.
Jenny	Dad comes from Scotland, doesn't he?
Mrs. Brown	That's right. He'll love these proverbs. Look.
Jenny	'A black hen lays a white egg.'* What does that mean?
Mrs. Brown	Don't worry. Your father will tell you.
Jenny	Here's another one: 'What may be done at any time will be done at no time.'* I can't make head or tail of it.
Mrs. Brown	Me neither. This will be just right for his birthday present.
Jenny	Mum. How about that Jacket? I think it's cool.
Mrs. Brown	Maybe next time. Let's go home.

* You can find the meaning of these proverbs in the Answer Key, at the back of the book.

Dialogue Quiz

1. What are Jenny and Mrs. Brown shopping for?
2. Do they know what they want to buy?
3. What does Mrs. Brown think about the purple jacket?
4. Where is the book department?
5. Where was Mr. Brown born?
6. Why can't Jenny understand the proverbs?

Debate Corner Us Groups

1. In your group (4 or 5 people), choose one of the motions below.

> 1. Proverbs help us solve our problems.
> 2. The grass is always greener on the other side of the hill.
> 3. Proverbs contain the culture of a country.
> 4. Ancient proverbs are no use in the 21st century.

2. Choose one pair (Pro) to agree with your motion, one pair (Con) to disagree with it, and (if there are 5 people in your group) one person to be the Timekeeper/Chairperson.

Pro/Con Pair, Speaker 1.
▶ These phrases will help you present your arguments:

Right?	Okay so far?	Let me give you an example.
You understand?	Have you got it?	To illustrate my point, …
Got me?	Know what I mean?	Please let me finish.
Got it?	For example, …	I haven't finished yet.
Are you following me?	For instance, …	I'm almost done.
Are you with me?	Take for example …	Hold on a second.

Pro/Con Pair, Speaker 2
▶ These phrases will help you to question the previous speaker:

Really?	Are you serious?	To get back to the point …
Is that right?	Go ahead.	To return to …
Are you sure?	You first.	In any case, …
How do you know?	I can wait.	Where was I?
Who told you that?	Never mind.	What were we talking about?
No way!	Anyway,	May I say something?

Timekeeper/Chairperson.
▶ These phrases will help you control the debate.

Today's motion is …	Speaking for the motion is ….
You have two minutes to speak.	Speaking against the motion is ….
Your time is up.	The next speaker is …
Next speaker please.	The motion has been accepted.
Your conclusions please.	The motion has been rejected.

Let's Prepare! Groups

- **Pro Pair/Con Pair:** Look at pages 62, 70, 86 and 102 for debate language and phrases. Then write three reasons for agreeing / disagreeing with the motion, plus your conclusion.
- There are some sample arguments on the next page.
- **Timekeeper/Chairperson:** Look at pages 72 and 102 for ideas and phrases.

First of all, ...

_____

_____

_____

Next, ...

_____

_____

_____

Furthermore, ...

_____

_____

_____

In conclusion, ...

_____

_____

_____

Let's Begin! Groups

- **Timekeeper/Chairperson:** Start the debate.
- Use the debate sample on page 72 and the phrases on page 102.
- Here is a checklist to help you.

1	Introduce yourself.	✔
2	State the motion.	
3	Introduce the speakers.	
4	Pro Speaker 1	
5	Con Speaker 1	
6	Questions from the floor	
7	Pro Speaker 2: Summary/Conclusion	
8	Con Speaker 2: Summary/Conclusion	
9	Vote	
10	Final remarks	

Proverbs 103

Argument Samples Us Groups

- Here are two samples to give you some ideas (Tracks 57 and 58).
- They are about the 4th motion 'Ancient proverbs are no use the 21st century'.
- Can you find phrases from page 102 in these samples?

Pro Speaker 1: I am in favor of the motion, for a number of reasons. To begin with, proverbs are all very well, but they're also very old. They don't tell us anything about today's problems. Are you with me? Nobody drove any cars in the old days and there were no TVs, cell phones, or computers. Know what I mean? Therefore We need to make some new proverbs to tell us what to do when the computer crashes, or when an email contains a virus. Let me give you an example: 'Backup or lose out' or 'When in doubt, delete.' Proverbs like these would be really useful! Right?

Con Speaker 1: You know what? I think proverbs are wonderful. Believe it or not, they tell us all about life. Even in our modern situation, we can always find proverbs which give us the answer. Right? To illustrate my point, when I see a new, shiny cell phone, it's good to remember that 'All that glitters is not gold.' When I can't do my homework, I can tell myself that 'Where there's a will, there's a way.' Let me tell you, I can't imagine how our ancestors managed to make so many great proverbs, but I'm very glad they did. Furthermore, their proverbs are timeless. Got it?

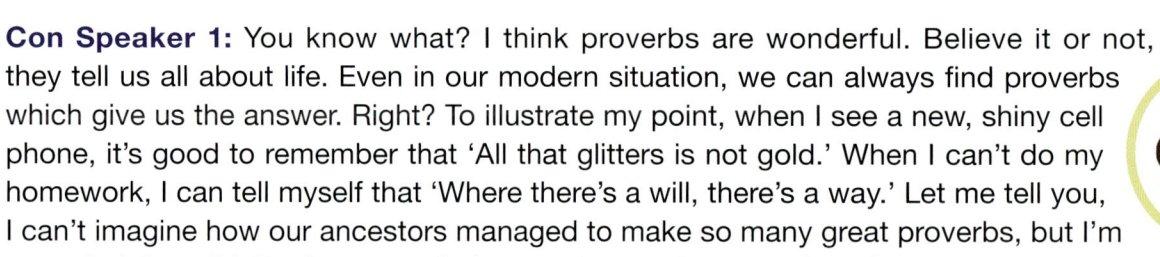

Hidden Proverbs Us 2

- Can you find the hidden proverbs that have been written on this wall?
- The answer is in the Answer Section at the back of the book.

104 Active English Discussion 2

Unit 13 News Media

Brainstorming
- Do you watch TV News?
- Do you read newspapers?
- Do you have a news feed on your phone?

Task 1

Headlines
- Look at these headlines together. When do you think these events happened?
- Write the headlines next to the dates, at the bottom of the page.

WORLD NEWS — Ban Ki-moon becomes UN Secretary General

SPORTS NEWS — ENGLAND WIN WORLD CUP

WORLD NEWS — FIRST MAN ON THE MOON

USA NEWS — MARTIN LUTHER KING SHOT

WORLD NEWS — TITANIC HIT BY ICEBERG

EUROPE NEWS — DIANA IS DEAD

USA NEWS — TWIN TOWERS COLLAPSE

BUSINESS NEWS — WALL STREET CRASH

SPORTS NEWS — KIM YUNA WINS GOLD MEDAL

April 16, 1912: _____
October 25, 1929: _____
July 30, 1966: _____
April 4, 1968: _____
July 21, 1969: _____
August 31, 1997: _____
September 11, 2001: _____
December 14, 2006: _____
February 25, 2010: _____

*The answers are in the Answer Key at the back of the book.

Breaking News

- Read this passage together and listen to Track 59.
- While you read, match the words and definitions at the bottom of the page.

 Groups

Are you interested in the news? Do you want to know what is happening in Korea? Do you want to know what is happening in the world? Thanks to satellite communication, news feeds and social networking services (SNS), news reports can be delivered to our tablets, laptops, PCs and phones. However, it hasn't always been that way.

Before the printing press was invented, news traveled by word of mouth. It was carried long distances by traders or messengers. In 490 BCE, a messenger ran 40 km from the plain of Marathon, to tell people in Athens about the Greek victory over the invading Persians. This gave birth to the Marathon event in the modern Olympic Games.

In Europe in the Middle Ages, handwritten newsletters appeared. However, it wasn't until 1666 that the first real English newspaper, The London Gazette, was published. Since then, the number of newspapers in the world has ballooned and modern printing presses print thousands of newspapers every hour.

These days, newspapers face competition from the Internet. Not only are there many online news sites, but a new type of reporting has appeared. This is done by ordinary people who are on the scene of events as they happen. They post videos on social media sites and these go viral. This means that anyone can now be a news reporter.

Match the words on the left to the definitions on the right.

breaking news	an ancient civilization, now the country of Iran
word of mouth	became very large very quickly
Persia	face-to-face communication; speaking
gave birth to	live events; up-to-date information
Middle Ages	seen by thousands of people in a short time
ballooned	started; initiated
viral	the period from about 1100 to 1453 in Europe

Further Reading: There are more reading passages at www.inkbooks.co.kr

Comprehension Check

1. How has modern technology affected the news?
2. What does 'SNS' mean?
3. How did news travel before the invention of the printing press?
4. What is the origin of the Marathon event in the Olympic Games?
5. When was the first English newspaper published?
6. What does 'go viral' mean?
7. How can we be news reporters?

Think for Yourself

- [ ] How many different types of news can you think of?
   (fashion news, movie news, current affairs, …)
- [ ] What other contents can you see in a newspaper?
- [ ] Are Korean news programs different from those in other countries?
- [ ] What is the breaking news at the moment?

Background Information

Did you know?

- [ ] If we go by number of readers, then 9 of the world's top 10 newspapers are in Asia.
- [ ] Here is a list of 'The 10 Best English Newspapers in the World':

   1. New York Times
   2. Washington Post
   3. Chicago Tribune
   4. Houston Chronicle
   5. San Francisco Chronicle
   6. Wall Street Journal
   7. The Guardian
   8. Financial Times
   9. Times of India
   10. The Daily Mail

- [ ] Almost 69% (9 million tons) of old newspapers in the United States are recycled.
- [ ] More than 24 billion newspapers are published every year.
- [ ] If all newspapers were recycled, this would save 250 million trees each year.
- [ ] Newspapers make almost all their money from advertisements.
- [ ] More than 4.2 billion people access SNSs on their mobile phones.

Discussion Groups

- Talk about the questions below.
- Use the **Conversation Strategies** at the bottom of the page.

1 What sort of news interests you most?
- ▶ International news or domestic news?
- ▶ Sporting news, fashion news, or entertainment news?
- ▶ Explain your preferences.

2 Do you talk about the news with your friends?
- ▶ Why? Why not? Support your opinion.

3 What's your favorite news media (TV, newspapers, Internet)?
- ▶ Explain the reason for your choice.

4 Would you like to be a news anchor?
- ▶ Why? Why not? Explain your reasons.

5 Would you like to be a news reporter?
- ▶ Why? Why not? Explain your thoughts.

6 What are the advantages and disadvantages of news media?
- ▶ Explain your thoughts.

7 Why do we see so many disasters and killings on TV news?
- ▶ Explain your opinion.

8 Do you believe everything you see on the news programs?
- ▶ Why? Why not? Support your opinion.

9 Do you agree with 'Freedom of the press'?
- ▶ Should newspapers be free from government pressure?
- ▶ Explain your ideas.

Conversation Strategies

Adding supporting statements:

Firstly, I think all censorship is wrong.	In addition, Furthermore, On top of that, What's more, And besides,	governments should not tell news channels what they can show.

108 Active English Discussion 2

Dialogue Us 2

Track 60

- Listen to Track 60 on the CD-Rom.
- Read the dialogue with your partner.
- Perform the dialogue together.
- Change roles. Perform the dialogue again.

(Jenny is surfing the Internet on her laptop, when Ji-hye enters the room)

Ji-hye   Hello Jenny? How's the homework going?

Jenny   Hi, Ji-hye. Actually, I got sidetracked into a news story.

Ji-hye   Really? Why's that?

Jenny   I was surfing for information for the assignment about tigers becoming endangered, and I found this story.

Ji-hye   What is it?

Jenny   Look, you can see the picture.

Ji-hye   Oh, yes. There's a mother dog with her 4 puppies.

Jenny   Look closer, Ji-hye.

Ji-hye   I can see they're all different colors, but so what?

Jenny   OK. I'll tell you. Three of them are tiger cubs.

Ji-hye   You're joking! Let me see again. Oh, yes.

Jenny   Their mother is in a zoo. She rejected them at birth.

Ji-hye   How could she do that? They're so cute.

Jenny   It's nice to see some good news online, isn't it?

Ji-hye   You're right. It makes a change.

Jenny   Now. Back to homework!

Key Words and Expressions

sidetracked
diverted; taken away from the topic

endangered
in danger of extinction

rejected at birth
The mother didn't want to look after the new-born cubs.

"It makes a change."
"It's nice to see something different."

Dialogue Quiz

1. Why was Jenny surfing the Internet?
2. Why did she get sidetracked?
3. Did Ji-hye understand the picture right away?
4. What mistake did she make?
5. Did the mother tiger want to take care of the tiger cubs?
6. Why does Ji-hye say 'It makes a change'?

News Reporter Role-play

- You are going to role-play a news report.
- What sort of news event will you report?

We will report about:

- Who will you interview?

We will interview:

- What questions will you ask?
- Here are some suggestions.
- The interview is on the next page.

Leah-Anne Thompson / Shutterstock.com

Let's Be Reporters!

- You have made a situation (page 110) and you have decided who to interview.
- Now you can make a script for your role-play.
- When you have finished, perform the role-play to another group.
- How about making a video?

Title:

Characters:

Location:

My Listening Skills

- When we discuss, we have to listen carefully to the speaker.
- How are your listening skills?
  1. Exchange books with your partner.
  2. Ask your partner the questions on this page.
  3. Mark your partner's answers in his/her book.

1 = Never, 2 = Almost never, 3 = Sometimes, 4 = Often, 5 = Always

#	When people talk to you, …	1	2	3	4	5
1	do you listen 100%?					
2	do you make eye contact?					
3	do you think of your answers?					
4	do you wait until the other person has finished?					
5	do you use positive body language?					
6	do you make sounds to show that you understand?					
7	do you nod your head to show that you understand.					
8	do you check that you understand ('Do you mean …?')?					
9	do you ask for repetition ('What did you say?') when you need it?					
10	do you ask them to speak slowly and clearly?					
11	do you listen in a friendly manner?					
12	do you try to cooperate with the speaker?					

My total out of 60 points is: ☐

Review

- Now review what you have done in this Unit and prepare for the next Unit.

Review — Browse the website for Unit 13.

Prepare — Look at the activities in Unit 14.

Preview — Browse the website for Unit 14.

Unit 14 Modern Life

Brainstorming

- How is modern life different from 100 years ago?
- How is it different from 10 years ago?
- How will it change in the next 10 years?

Task 1

Telling the Future
- Think about possible changes in the next 10 years.
- Check the boxes that match your opinion.

1 = No way, 2 = Maybe, 3 = Yes, absolutely.

	In the next ten years, …	1	2	3
1	… all transport (trains, buses, planes) will use clean fuel.			
2	… there will be a cure for cancer.			
3	… there will be no schools. Students will study online.			
4	… there will be tourists on the moon.			
5	… headphones will translate any language into Korean.			
6	… there will be no poverty in the world.			
7	… there will be no wars in the world.			
8	… South Korea and North Korea will unify.			
9	… cars will all drive themselves. People will be passengers.			

Task 2

What Do You Think?
- What do you think will happen in your lifetime?
- Write your ideas in the table below. (Science, travel, pollution, weather, AI, space, etc.)
- Ask people in other groups whether they agree or disagree.

We think that in our lifetime, …	No way	Maybe	Yes
1.			
2.			
3.			
4.			

A Better Place

- Read this passage together and listen to Track 61.
- While you read, match the words and definitions at the bottom of the page.

 Groups

If we had been born 200 years ago, we might have gone to school, but not to university. There was no electricity and oil lamps were used at night. In addition, there were no cars or telephones, so travel was mostly on foot and communication was very difficult. The average age for marriage at that time was 15. Now it is 29 for women and 32 for men.

These days, we have satellites, jet planes, trains, cars, cell phones, the Internet, email, and many more things that our ancestors couldn't even dream of. Furthermore, 80% of Koreans now live in cities, many of them in tall apartment buildings. The quality of life has improved enormously, and the average life expectancy has reached 82, compared with 47.5 in 1955.

However, it is important to ask whether the changes have all been positive. For example, pollution and fossil fuels have given us global warming. Average temperatures are rising, and extreme weather is becoming common. Modern medicine helps us to live longer, but Korean is now an 'aged' society, since 14% of its people are over 65.

All in all, it is difficult to imagine what the world will look like 200 years later. What we can say is that it is up to us to make it a better place for our descendants. As the UNICEF ambassador Liam Neeson has said, 'The cause of making the world a better place for children unites us all'.

Match the words on the left to the definitions on the right.

- quality of life • • fuels made from oil, gas or coal
- enormously • • hugely; largely; greatly
- life expectancy • • severe or unseasonal weather
- fossil fuels • • the number of years one can expect to live
- global warming • • the rate of comfort; the enjoyment value of life
- extreme weather • • increase in the temperature of the earth
- descendant • • a person related to people born in the past
- ambassador • • a high-level representative

Comprehension Check

1. How was life different 200 years ago?
2. How did people get from town to town?
3. How has the quality of life improved?
4. How long could you expect to live if you were born in 1955?
5. Has progress had only good results?
6. What are some of the problems of modern life?
7. What is the conclusion of this passage?

Think for Yourself

- [ ] Can you imagine living 200 years ago?
- [ ] Can you imagine living 200 years in the future?
- [ ] Talk to your parents when you are at home.
   ▸ How was life different when they were children?
- [ ] What do the letters UNICEF stand for?

Background Information

Did you know?

- [ ] The longest recorded life was that of Jeanne Louise Calment of France (1875–1997), who was 122 when she died. She met Vincent van Gogh when she was 14 years old.
- [ ] In 1850 the life expectancy of white males in the USA was 40. By 2014 this figure had almost doubled to 77.
- [ ] 2016 was the warmest year since records began, in 1880.
- [ ] The next 4 hottest years were: 2015, 2014, 2010 and 2013.
- [ ] The world population doubled in the 36 years from 1970 to 2016, when it reached 7.4 billion.
- [ ] The world's population is increasing at the rate of 83 million people per year and is expected to reach 9 billion by 2040.
- [ ] In 2014 there were 1 billion motor vehicles in the world. This is expected to rise to 2 billion by 2035.
- [ ] The sea level has risen by 10 to 25 cms over the last 100 years.
- [ ] 1/3 of the earth's land surface is changing into deserts (desertification), affecting nearly one billion people.

Discussion Us Groups

- Talk about the questions below.
- Use the **Conversation Strategies** at the bottom of the page.

1 What do you like about the modern world?
  ▶ Talk about your opinion.

2 What don't you like about the modern world?
  ▶ Explain your opinion.

3 Do you think the quality of life will be better in 50 years?
  ▶ Why? Why not? Support your opinion.

4 Will robots replace humans in the future?
  ▶ Explain your thoughts.

5 Will space travel become possible?
  ▶ Tell us about your opinion.

6 Would you like to live on another planet?
  ▶ Why? Why not?

7 How can we deal with global warming?
  ▶ Explain your ideas.

8 What is the biggest problem in the world today?
  ▶ What can we do about that problem?

9 If you could travel back in time, which year would you choose to visit?
  ▶ Why? Talk about it together.

10 If you were Secretary General of the United Nations, what would you do?
  ▶ What would you ask wealthy countries to do?
  ▶ How would you help developing countries?

Conversation Strategies

Giving unpleasant information:

In fact, Actually, Frankly speaking, To be honest, To tell the truth, Have you heard?	the sea level is rising by 1 cm every 10 years.

Expressing disbelief:

Are you sure? Who told you that? Come on now. Come off it. Be realistic. Be serious.	You must be joking. You're pulling my leg.

Dialogue

- Listen to Track 62 on the CD-Rom.
- Read the dialogue with your partner.
- Perform the dialogue together.
- Change roles. Perform the dialogue again.

(Kevin is outside the house, on the lawn. Ji-hye sees him and comes up to him.)

Ji-hye	Hey, Kevin. What's that?
Kevin	Hi, Ji-hye. It's a weather station.
Ji-hye	What's that? I'm not with you.
Kevin	Well, there's a thermometer for measuring temperature, a barometer for measuring air-pressure, a wind gauge, and a rain gauge.
Ji-hye	OK, but why are you doing this?
Kevin	I'm interested in climate change.
Ji-hye	You mean global warming?
Kevin	That's right. I want to see if I can measure it myself.
Ji-hye	To be honest, I don't see what all the fuss is about.
Kevin	Really? What about all the extreme weather these days?
Ji-hye	Well, we don't really know what causes it.
Kevin	And what about the rising sea level?
Ji-hye	Let's just say I'm not sure.
Kevin	Why don't you help me? Then we'll find out.
Ji-hye	OK. Let's do it.

Key Words and Expressions

weather station
a box containing instruments for measuring the weather

gauge
a measuring instrument

climate change
long term changes in the weather

fuss
argument, discussion, trouble

Dialogue Quiz

1. What is Kevin doing?
2. What aspects of the weather will he measure?
3. Why does Kevin want to measure the weather?
4. What does Ji-hye think about climate change?
5. Does Kevin agree with Ji-hye?
6. What does Kevin suggest?

Debate Corner Groups

1. In your group (4 or 5 people), choose one of the motions below.

> 1. This is the best time to be alive.
> 2. Our grandchildren will enjoy a much better world.
> 3. Global problems are now too difficult to solve.
> 4. Our ancestors had a better quality of life.

2. Choose one pair (Pro) to agree with your motion, one pair (Con) to disagree with it, and (if there are 5 people in your group) one person to be the Timekeeper/Chairperson.

Pro/Con Pair, Speaker 1
▶ These phrases will help you present your arguments:

Do you believe that …?	What do you think of …?	The best way is …
Do you think we should …?	There are exceptions.	We really have to …
Would you consider …?	This does include …	Alternatively, …
Are you for or against …?	Except, of course …	Instead, …
Would you prefer …?	One exception is …	On the other hand, …
Would you rather …?	The solution is …	There again, …

Pro/Con Pair, Speaker 2
▶ These phrases will help you to question the previous speaker:

Don't they …?	Why shouldn't they?	In that case,
Don't you think that …?	What if …?	In that respect,
Don't you see that …?	What happens if …?	As far as that goes,
Can't you see that …?	If that is so …,	On that point, …
Wouldn't it be better to …?	You would be right if …	You lost me there.
Wouldn't you agree that …?	That would make sense if …	I'm not following.

Timekeeper/Chairperson
▶ These phrases will help you control the debate.

Today's motion is …	Speaking for the motion is ….
You have two minutes to speak.	Speaking against the motion is ….
Your time is up.	The next speaker is …
Next speaker please.	The motion has been accepted.
Your conclusions please.	The motion has been rejected.

Let's Prepare! Groups

- **Pro Pair/Con Pair:** Look at pages 62, 70, 86, 102 and 118 for debate language. Then write three reasons for agreeing with the motion, plus your conclusion.
- There are some sample arguments on the next page.
- **Timekeeper/Chairperson:** Look at pages 72 and 118 for ideas and phrases.

First of all, …
_____
_____
_____

Next, …
_____
_____
_____

What's more, …
_____
_____
_____

In conclusion, …
_____
_____
_____

Let's Begin! Groups

- **Timekeeper/Chairperson:** Start the debate.
- Use the debate sample on page 72 and the phrases on page 118.
- Here is a checklist to help you.

1	Introduce yourself.	✔
2	State the motion.	
3	Introduce the speakers.	
4	Pro Speaker 1	
5	Con Speaker 1	
6	Questions from the floor	
7	Pro Speaker 2: Summary/Conclusion	
8	Con Speaker 2: Summary/Conclusion	
9	Vote	
10	Final remarks	

Modern Life

Argument Samples Us Groups

- Here are two samples to give you some ideas (Tracks 63 and 64).
- They are about the first motion on page 118: 'This is the best time to be alive'.
- Can you find phrases from page 118 in these samples?

Pro Speaker 1: I'm really glad that I was born in the modern world. Let me give you three reasons for this. Firstly, thanks to advanced technology, I can watch movies, travel by jet plane, surf the Internet and call my friends on my cell phone. Can you imagine living without these? Second, the quality of life is better than it has ever been. people are living much longer and happier lives thanks to modern medicine. Third, we have freedom of speech and we can read, watch and do whatever we like - as long as it's legal. This is as good as it gets. Do you really think it could get any better?

Con Speaker 1: Do you believe that the previous speaker knows what he's talking about? Wouldn't you agree that he's talking out of the back of his head? To begin with, advanced technology has brought all sorts of problems, including pollution, global warming, nuclear weapons and man-made disasters. Next, there seem to be even more epidemics such as SARS, MERS and Ebola, despite modern medicine. Finally, can't you see that our emails and text messages are being monitored? Furthermore, we are always being watched on CCTV cameras. In that respect, this is not freedom of speech. As far as that goes, this is definitely not the best time to be alive.

Reflection Me

- How are your teamwork skills?
- There are no correct answers. Just write about yourself.

My Teamwork Skills	
Cooperation	
Communication	
Contribution	
Conflict Management	
Leadership	

There are more activities on the website at www.inkbooks.co.kr.

Unit 15 Relationships

Brainstorming

- What do you think about relationships?
- Do you want to get married?
- Do you want to stay single?

Task

Relationship Crossword
- Look at these clues and solve this crossword together.
- The answers are in the Answer Key, at the back of the book.

What do you think?

How do you spell it?

What's 4 Across?

What does it mean?

What's 3 Down?

How many letters?

Across

1 'We've had our ups and _ _ _ _ _ _.'
4 'We don't always see eye to _ _ _.'
6 'They are well _ _ _ _ _ _ _ _.'
11 'It was love at first _ _ _ _ _.'
12 'He popped the _ _ _ _ _ _ _ _ last night.'
14 'They have a lot in _ _ _ _ _ _.'
15 _ _ _ _ _ _ _ _ _ _ love (one-sided love)
18 _ _ _ _ _ _ _ _ _'s Day is February 14th.
20 'We fell head over _ _ _ _ _ in love.'

Down

2 'I'm not ready to _ _ _ _ _ _ down yet.'
3 A close relationship with no romance
5 'We _ _ _ _ out after an argument.'
7 'We enjoy each other's _ _ _ _ _ _ _ _.'
8 'We're just good _ _ _ _ _ _ _ _.'
9 'We get on like a house on _ _ _ _.'
10 'We soon _ _ _ _ _ _ up a relationship.'
13 'He is my _ _ _ _ _ _ _ _ _ _ _ other.'
16 'They go back _ _ _ _ _.'
17 'We've been going _ _ _ _ _ _ for a while.'
19 'We get on _ _ _ _ together.'

Modern Relationships

- Read this passage together and listen to Track 65.
- While you read, match the words and definitions at the bottom of the page.

Us Groups

Not long ago everyone expected to get married, settle down and have a family. However, things are different these days. The number of marriages is decreasing and the average age of those who do tie the knot has risen from 27.8 (men) and 24.8 (women) in 1990 to 32.4 and 29.8 in 2014. Furthermore, the number of couples in which the woman is older than the man has increased by 10,000 over the last 10 years.

These trends have been blamed on economic reasons. Men talk about unstable employment and women cite the cost of the wedding ceremony. These factors gave birth to the 'Sampo' generation, who have given up their dreams of relationships, marriage and having a child. Then came the 'Chilpo' generation, and most recently, the 'N-po' generation, who have given up more things that they can count.

One of the problems is that parenting is very expensive. Bringing up a child until it enters university costs more than 200 million Korean Won. This is a conservative figure, since it doesn't include education at private institutes (*hagwons*).

Not surprisingly, some young people are choosing to stay single and pursue their careers. Some even have 'single bride' photo shoots instead of a real wedding. Others are advocating cohabitation without marriage. All in all, these trends add up to changes in the traditional values of Korean society. We might well ask 'What's next?'

Match the words on the left to the definitions on the right.

tie the knot	a social event
unstable	cause; result in
cite	follow; be involved in
ceremony	get married
give birth to	likely to change; not secure
conservative	living together
pursue	probably lower than the actual figure
advocate	refer to; mention
cohabitation	support; argue for

Further Reading: There are more reading passages at www.inkbooks.co.kr

Comprehension Check

1. What was the average of women who married in 1990?
2. What was the average of men who married in 2014?
3. Why has the average marriage age risen?
4. What have the 'Sampo' generation given up?
5. What have the 'N-po' generation given up?
6. How much does it cost to raise a child?
7. What is the conclusion this passage?

Think for Yourself

- [ ] Why do people get married?
- [ ] Why do people get divorced?
- [ ] What is the best way to find a lifelong partner?
- [ ] Do you agree with arranged marriages?

Background Information

Did you know?

- [ ] According to a Dong-a Ilbo report of 2015, 70% of Koreans in their 20-30s thought it was OK to marry a foreigner.
- [ ] 61% thought that cohabitation was acceptable.
- [ ] Only 9% thought it was 'imperative' to get married.
- [ ] In 2011 the average cost of getting married, including the reception, gifts, home furnishings and honeymoon, was 208 million Korean Won.
- [ ] 40% of women in the USA think a man's education is more important than his looks.
- [ ] 29% of women in the USA spend more time buying shoes than looking for a husband.
- [ ] Dating is not allowed until the age of 15 in South America.
- [ ] Dating is against the law in Iran.
- [ ] Over 20 million people visit online dating services each month.
- [ ] National Singles Week in the U.S. is the 3rd week in September.
- [ ] According to a survey of single people, Wednesday is the best day for a first date.

Discussion Groups

- Talk about the questions below.
- Use the **Conversation Strategies** at the bottom of the page.

1 Do you intend to get married?
  ▶ Why? Why not? Explain your ideas.

2 What do you think of international marriages?
  ▶ Explain your opinion.

3 Do you believe in 'love at first sight'?
  ▶ Why? Why not? Support your opinion.

4 Is it OK if a girl invites a boy on a date?
  ▶ Why? Why not? Support your opinion.

5 Should the boy be older than the girl?
  ▶ Explain your opinion.

6 Would you let your parents choose your future spouse?
  ▶ Why? Why not? Tell us your opinion.

7 Can a man and a woman just be good friends?
  ▶ Explain your ideas.

8 What do you think about cohabitation?
  ▶ Support your opinion.

9 What do you think of single parent families?
  ▶ Support your opinion.

10 What do you think of gay marriage?
  ▶ Support your opinion.

Conversation Strategies

Expressing an opinion:	Agreeing:	Disagreeing:
In my opinion …	I agree.	I disagree.
If you ask me, …	I couldn't agree more.	I can't agree.
I think that …	Me too.	Oh, I don't think so.
I believe that …	So do I.	Oh, I don't believe that.
I don't like …	Me neither.	Oh, I do.
I don't believe in …	Neither do I.	Oh, I wouldn't say that.

Dialogue

- Listen to Track 66 on the CD-Rom.
- Read the dialogue with your partner.
- Perform the dialogue together.
- Change roles. Perform the dialogue again.

Track 66

Key Words and Expressions

nobody
"nobody you know" "nobody important"

broke up
finished the relationship

ask out
ask for a date

"You never know."
"Who knows?"
"Anything is possible."
"Anything can happen."

(Seung-min is talking on the phone, when Mrs. Brown enters the room)

Seung-min	OK, bye. See you tonight. *(He puts the phone down.)*
Mrs. Brown	Hello, Seung-min.
Seung-min	Good morning, Mrs. Brown.
Mrs. Brown	Who was that on the phone?
Seung-min	Oh, nobody. I only met her a few days ago.
Mrs. Brown	I thought you had a girlfriend.
Seung-min	Yes, but we broke up last week.
Mrs. Brown	I see. And what about that other girl you used to talk about?
Seung-min	Oh, her. She's too good for me.
Mrs. Brown	What do you mean?
Seung-min	She wouldn't even think of dating me.
Mrs. Brown	How do you know, if you never ask her?
Seung-min	I'm too shy to ask her out.
Mrs. Brown	You never know. Maybe she likes you!
Seung-min	Do you think so?

Dialogue Quiz

1. Who was Seung-min talking to on the phone?
2. What happened to his previous girlfriend?
3. Who would he really like to date?
4. Why doesn't he ask her for a date?
5. What advice does Mrs. Brown give to Seung-min?
6. Why does Mrs. Brown say 'You never know'?

Relationship Role-play Groups

- You are going to make a role-play about relationships.
- What sort of role-play will you make?
- Here are some ideas and situations:

1. International Marriage
A family meeting between the father, mother, son and daughter. The son wants to marry a non-Korean girlfriend. What does the mother think? What does the father think? How about the daughter? What will happen?

2. Arranged Meeting
The parents have arranged a meeting for the son. He goes to the meeting to see the girl. What happens? Do they get on? Do they agree to meet again, or do they part? What does the son say to the parents? What do they say to him?

3. Love Triangle
A and B both love C. What will happen? Will A and B confess their love to C? What will C say? Will A and B have a fight? Perhaps C loves another person. What is the ending to the story? Will they live happily ever after?

4. Schoolfriend Reunion
Some school friends get together. They haven't seen each other for 10 years. Maybe one is married with children, one is still single, one is divorced, one has lived abroad, and so on. What will they say to each other? What will happen?

5. Just Good Friends
A couple have been close friends for a long time. One of them has romantic feelings, but the other wants to stay single and follow his/her career. He/she values their friendship. What will they say to each other? What will happen in the end?

- These are ideas for the role-play.
- However, you can use your own ideas.
- Use the storyboard on the next page for the plot of your role-play.
- Try to use the conversation strategies you have learned in Units 1 to 15.
- How about making a video? Perhaps one person in the group could be the director/cameraman.

Role-play Storyboard Us Groups

- Make a storyboard for your role-play.
- Perform your role-play together.
- Now perform it to another group or make a video.

Title: _____

Relationships 127

My Discussion Skills

- You have been discussing, role-playing and debating for 15 Units.
- How are your oral performance skills now?
  1. Exchange books with your partner.
  2. Ask your partner the questions on this page.
  3. Mark your partner's answers in his/her book.

1 = No, not at all - 0%, **2** = No, not really - 25%, **3** = Yes, sort of - 50%, **4** = Yes, OK - 75%, **5** = Yes - 100%.

What can you do now?	1	2	3	4	5
Can you talk about friendship? (Unit 1)					
Can you talk about favorites? (Unit 2)					
Can you talk about movies? (Unit 3)					
Can you give and receive advice? (Unit 4)					
Are you more confident about your speaking? (Unit 5)					
Can you talk about a healthy diet? (Unit 6)					
Can you talk about studying abroad? (Unit 7)					
Can you talk about art and music? (Unit 8)					
Can you talk about Internet shopping? (Unit 9)					
Can you talk about traffic? (Unit 10)					
Can you talk about culture shock? (Unit 11)					
Can you talk about proverbs? (Unit 12)					
Can you talk about news media? (Unit 13)					
Can you talk about modern life? (Unit 14)					
Can you talk about relationships? (Unit 15)					
My total out of 75 points is:					

- Take some time to think about your discussion skills.
- What can you do now that you couldn't do at the start?
- How have you improved?
- What do you need to do now?

Unit 16 Progress

Brainstorming

- What are the best inventions ever?
- What things help us most in our life?
- How have we progressed since 100 years ago?

Task 1 — Inventions

- Here is a list of popular inventions.
- Can you match the inventions with their descriptions?
- How would you rank these inventions, from 1 to 10?

Rank	Inventions	Descriptions
____	Penicillin	This gives us a network of communication.
____	The Television	This puts words on the page.
____	The Automobile	This performs calculations very quickly.
____	The Camera	This gives us entertainment in our homes.
____	The Computer	This captures images.
____	The Printing Press	This is a method of private transport.
____	The Light Bulb	This changes electricity into light.
____	The Internet	This transmits your voice.
____	The Steam Engine	This cures infections and diseases.
____	The Telephone	This powered the first trains.

The solution is in the Answer Key, at the back of the book.

Task 2 — Alphabetical Inventions

- Can you think of an invention for every letter of the alphabet?
- Talk together. Brainstorm!
- Some inventions have been filled in to get you started.

Air Balloon	B	C	D
E	Film	G	H
I	J	Keyboard	L
M	N	O	Paper Clip
QWERTY	R	S	T
U	Volleyball	W	X
Y	Z		

A suggested solution is in the Answer Key, at the back of the book.

Save the World

- Read this passage together and listen to Track 67.
- While you read, match the words and definitions at the bottom of the page.

The Age of Enlightenment (1715 - 1789) was also the time of the Scientific Revolution, when great advances were made in mathematics, physics, astronomy, biology and chemistry. This in turn led to the Industrial Revolution (1760 - 1840), which affected every aspect of daily life, through the development of water power, steam power and factory methods of manufacturing.

During the Industrial Revolution machines started to replace hand-labor. People moved to the cities to work in the factories. They hoped to improve their standard of living this way. However, the coal used in the steam engines produced thick smog. What's more, poor children had to work in the factories, in terrible conditions.

More recently, the Digital Revolution has given us satellite communication, computers, the Internet and other amazing inventions. Medical science has also helped people to live longer. On the other hand, this progress has resulted in global warming, pollution and overpopulation. The world's water is being used up, deserts are getting bigger, forests are being cut down, and seas are being overfished.

Now is the time to think about 'sustainable development.' Instead of using up the world's natural resources, we need to use renewable energy, like sunlight, wind-power, and wave-power. We need to conserve water, build up fish stocks and plant new forests. Surely, the next step in the progress of mankind (and womankind) is to take care of our world. It's the only one we have!

Match the words on the left to the definitions on the right.

standard of living	able to be replaced naturally
smog	growth that doesn't use up the world's resources
global warming	polluted air from factories
overpopulation	prevent loss or waste
overfishing	taking all the fish from the seas
sustainable development	the degree of wealth and comfort
natural resources	the overcrowding of the world
renewable	the rise in world temperatures
conserve	things in and on the earth, used by humans

Further Reading: There are more reading passages at www.inkbooks.co.kr

Comprehension Check

1. What happened in the Age of Enlightenment?
2. What were the advantages of the Industrial Revolution?
3. What were the disadvantages of the Industrial Revolution?
4. What are the advantages of the Digital Revolution?
5. What are the disadvantages of the Digital Revolution?
6. How many natural resources can you find in this passage?
7. How many sources of renewable energy can you find in this passage?

Think for Yourself

- [ ] Is progress always good?
- [ ] Could you live without computers, smartphones, and SNSs?
- [ ] Can you think of other examples of progress?
- [ ] What do you think the world will look like in 50 years' time?

Background Information

Did you know?

- [ ] Alfred Nobel was the inventor of dynamite. He was sad that this invention was used for killing people, so he made the Nobel Peace Prize, which is awarded each year.
- [ ] Ernest Hamwi made the ice cream cone in 1904 in St. Louis, USA, when an ice cream seller ran out of dishes.
- [ ] The 4th Earl of Sandwich (1718-1792) loved playing cards so much that he didn't want to leave the gaming table to eat his meals. Instead, he told his cook to put his food between two slices of bread, which he ate while playing.
- [ ] The first traffic lights in the world were installed in Detroit, in 1920.
- [ ] President Theodore Roosevelt (1858-1919) was on a hunting trip in Mississippi in November 1902. His men found a black bear cub for him to shoot, but he set it free. The 'Teddy Bear' was born because of this event.
- [ ] Blue jeans were invented in 1873 by Jacob Davis and Levi Strauss. They were originally called Waist Overalls.
- [ ] The first touchscreen was invented in the UK in 1965.

Discussion Us ▶ Groups

- Talk about the questions below.
- Use the **Conversation Strategies** at the bottom of the page.

1 What do you think is the best invention ever?

2 What do you think is the worst invention ever?

3 Do you know any stories about famous inventors?
▶ Tell everyone about them.

4 Do you think time machines will ever be invented?
▶ Explain your ideas. Why do you think that way?

5 What do you think of cloning?
▶ Explain your thoughts.

6 What do you think of genetically modified (GM) foods?
▶ Explain your opinion.

7 Is the world a better place than it was 100 years ago?
▶ Why? Why not? Support your opinion.

8 Will the world be a better place in 100 years' time?
▶ Why? Why not? Explain your opinion.

9 How can our quality of life be improved in the future?
▶ Explain your ideas.

10 How can we get rid of poverty and hunger?
▶ Explain your opinion.

11 Do you think science can solve every problem in the world?
▶ Explain your opinion.

Conversation Strategies

Agreeing:	Disagreeing:
Right.	You have a point, but …
I agree.	I'm not sure I agree.
That's true.	I disagree, on the whole.
I know what you mean.	I can't agree with you.
I couldn't agree more.	I think you're wrong.
You're absolutely right.	That's not correct.
You hit the nail on the head.	I disagree.

Dialogue

- Listen to Track 68 on the CD-Rom.
- Read the dialogue with your partner.
- Perform the dialogue together.
- Change roles. Perform the dialogue again.

Key Words and Expressions

"No kidding?"
"Is that so?"
"Is that true?"

"We've paid a price."
"There have been disadvantages as well as advantages."

"It makes you think."
"That's food for thought!"
"That's something to think about!"

(Jenny enters the living room, where Mr. Brown is reading.)

Jenny	Hi, dad! What are you reading?
Mr. Brown	Hello, Jenny. It's a book about the Industrial Revolution.
Jenny	Really? Isn't that boring?
Mr. Brown	Well, Jenny, if you were working in a cotton factory, you wouldn't be bored. You'd be hungry, tired and sick.
Jenny	No kidding?
Mr. Brown	It's the truth. Children even went down coal mines.
Jenny	That can't be right.
Mr. Brown	I'm afraid it is. And you'd probably only live till you were 40.
Jenny	40? But you're much older than that!
Mr. Brown	Not too much! But I'm an old man for those times.
Jenny	That's amazing. We've really progressed since then.
Mr. Brown	Yes, though we've paid a price.
Jenny	What do you mean?
Mr. Brown	We have longer lives, but we also have pollution, global warming and overpopulation.
Jenny	I suppose you're right. It certainly makes you think!

Dialogue Quiz

1. What is Mr. Brown doing?
2. Is Jenny tired? Is she sick?
3. Is Mr. Brown joking?
4. What was the average life expectancy during the Industrial Revolution?
5. What are the disadvantages of progress?
6. Does Jenny still think the topic is boring at the end of the dialogue?

Debate Corner Groups

1. In your group (4 or 5 people), choose one of the motions below.

> 1. Tradition prevents progress.
> 2. Progress should help the rich and the poor.
> 3. Progress has too many harmful side effects.
> 4. Humankind's best days are ahead of us.

2. Choose one pair (Pro) to agree with your motion, one pair (Con) to disagree with it, and (if there are 5 people in your group) one person to be the Timekeeper/Chairperson.

Pro/Con Pair, Speaker 1
▶ These phrases will help you present and conclude your arguments:

We strongly believe the motion is true.	There are many examples for this.
Let us first define some terms.	You can find many examples.
What do we mean by …. ?	So we can see clearly that …
First of all, I will talk about …	So as we have seen, …
The second speaker will talk about …	Now because of this, ….
My first argument is …	We ask you to support this motion.

Pro/Con Pair, Speaker 2
▶ These phrases help you question the previous speaker and conclude your argument:

Let us look at what … has said.	Wouldn't you agree that … ?
The first speaker has told us that …	I'm going to come to that point.
On the contrary, …	As the first speaker has told you, …
He/she also said that …	I'd like to summarize our argument.
But in fact, …	I beg you to oppose the motion.
We oppose the motion because …	For these reasons the motion must fail.

Timekeeper/Chairperson
▶ These phrases help you control the debate.

Today's motion is …	Speaking for the motion is ….
You have two minutes to speak.	Speaking against the motion is ….
Your time is up.	The next speaker is …
Next speaker please.	The motion has been accepted.
Your conclusions please.	The motion has been rejected.

Let's Prepare! Us Groups

- **Pro Pair/Con Pair:** Look at pages 62, 70, 86, 102, 118 and 134 for debate language. Then write three reasons for agreeing with the motion, plus your conclusion.
- There are some sample arguments on the next page.
- **Timekeeper/Chairperson:** Look at pages 72 and 134 for ideas and phrases.

First of all, ...
_____
_____
_____

Next, ...
_____
_____
_____

What's more, ...
_____
_____
_____

In conclusion, ...
_____
_____
_____

Let's Begin! Us Groups

- **Timekeeper/Chairperson:** Start the debate.
- Use the debate sample on page 72 and the phrases on page 134.
- Here is a checklist to help you.

1	Introduce yourself.	✓
2	State the motion.	
3	Introduce the speakers.	
4	Pro Speaker 1	
5	Con Speaker 1	
6	Questions from the floor	
7	Pro Speaker 2: Summary/Conclusion	
8	Con Speaker 2: Summary/Conclusion	
9	Vote	
10	Final remarks	

Progress 135

Argument Samples Groups

Tracks 69 and 70

- Here are two samples to give you some ideas (Tracks 69 and 70).
- They are about motion number 4: 'Humankind's best days are ahead of us.'
- Can you find phrases from page 134 in these samples?

Pro Speaker 1: We strongly believe the motion is true. We can see clearly that our standard of living is much better than 100, 50, or even 20 years ago, and it's going to get better. My argument is that science and technology have made our lives much more comfortable. Because of this we can browse the Internet, turn on the TV, watch a movie, and travel to anywhere in the world. What's more, thanks to medical science, we live much longer than our ancestors did. Finally, science is always progressing. Our grandchildren can look forward to a golden age.

Con Speaker 1: The first speaker has told us that life is getting better all the time. But in fact, when it comes to technology, too many people are wearing rose-colored glasses. On the contrary, if they look around, they'll see pollution, global warming, over-population, and high-technology war. Furthermore, they'll see poverty and hunger in the poor countries that have not been helped by progress. Wouldn't you agree that it's time to face facts? We have to start looking after the world, before it's too late. Otherwise humankind's best days are behind us. I therefore beg you to oppose the motion.

Save The World Puzzle 2

- Can you arrange the letters correctly in these posters?
- The answers are in the Answer Section at the back of the book.

edreuc
ruees
elrccey

aves weart

yerev drpo
tcsoun

tanlp a eter

pntal a file

tcshwi fof

asve yenreg

vsea eht arhet

st'rhee on lcpae klie oh!me

Unit 17 Konglish

Brainstorming

- What is Konglish?
- Where does it come from?
- Is it OK to use Konglish?

Task 1
- How many Konglish words can you think of?
- Write them below. (Some have been added for you.)

> eye shopping   blues dance
>
> arbeit   fighting!

Task 2
- There are many types of Englishes in the world. Here are some of them.
- Where do you think they come from?

Banglish _____	Italglish _____	Shanglish _____
Chinglish _____	Japlish _____	Singlish _Singapore_
Finglish _____	Manglish _____	Spanglish _____
Franglaish _____	Paklish _____	Thaiglish _____
Inglish _____	Runglish _____	Wenglish _____

The answers can be found in the Answer Key, at the back of the book.

World Englishes

- Read this passage together and listen to Track 71.
- While you read, match the words and definitions at the bottom of the page.

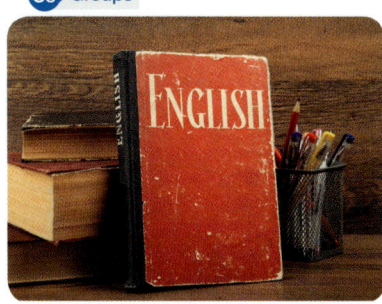

During the reign of Queen Victoria (1837-1901), it was said that the sun never set on the British Empire. Since that time, the Empire has disappeared, but its language has continued to spread round the world. What began as a second language (ESL) or a foreign language (EFL), soon became an international language (EIL) and is now a global language (EGL).

Up to now, it was thought that the best people to teach English were 'native speakers.' However, this view is changing. English has become a common language of business, research and communication. People using this 'lingua franca' do not need difficult idioms or 'standard' pronunciation. They simply want to understand each other. Bilingual teachers from their own countries are perfect for this, since they understand the needs and problems of the learners.

Another important change is the rise of Regional Englishes such as Konglish, Chinglish and Japlish. These were thought to be 'wrong' at first and books were written to correct their 'mistakes.' These days, however, Konglish is respected as a World English. It allows the speakers to express their own cultural ideas, rather than western ones.

As time goes by, more and more people are learning English at younger and younger ages. Nevertheless, we must not forget the importance of the mother tongue. Luckily, the Korean language is gaining in popularity around the world, thanks to the Korean Wave, or Hallyu. Rather than being an endangered language, Korean is holding its own in this era of global English.

Match the words on the left to the definitions on the right.

native speakers	a common language used by people around the world
lingua franca	a way of speaking that experts think is correct
standard pronunciation	a speaker's native language
bilingual	able to speak two language equally well
Regional Englishes	local varieties of English
mother tongue	one used by fewer and fewer people; almost extinct
endangered language	people whose mother tongue is English
holding its own	surviving; not declining

Further Reading: There are more reading passages at www.inkbooks.co.kr

Comprehension Check

1. When did Queen Victoria reign?
2. What does 'the sun never set' mean?
3. What does 'EIL' mean?
4. What does 'EGL' mean?
5. Why are bilingual teachers perfect for EFL learners?
6. Why is Konglish respected?
7. What is the conclusion of this passage?

Think for Yourself

- [ ] What do you think of Konglish?
- [ ] Can you understand native speakers of English?
- [ ] Have you ever heard people speaking Japlish or Chinglish?

Background Information

Did you know?

- [ ] There are 196 countries in the world and over 7,000 spoken languages. However, 2,000 of these have fewer than 1,000 speakers.
- [ ] In the year 1500, there were about 1,400 languages and in the year 2100 there will be about 4,000.
- [ ] A language dies every two weeks (livingtongues.org).
- [ ] 12 languages are spoken by 50% of the world's population.
- [ ] The most commonly used language in the world is Mandarin. It is spoken by over 1.3 billion people (native speakers).
- [ ] The next most common languages (native speakers) are:
  - Spanish (427 million)
  - Arabic (267 million)
  - Portuguese (202 million)
  - Russian (171 million)
  - Javanese (84 million)
  - English (339 million)
  - Hindi (260 million)
  - Bengali (189 million)
  - Japanese (128 million)
  - Korean (77.3 million)
- [ ] In 2014 there were more than a billion people learning English.
- [ ] There could be around 2 billion people learning English as a second language by 2020.

Discussion — Groups

- Talk about the questions below.
- Use the **Conversation Strategies** at the bottom of the page.

1. If you could speak another language (apart from English), which one would you choose?
   - ▶ Why? Explain your reasons.

2. What do you think about Konglish, Japlish, Chinglish, etc.?
   - ▶ Explain your ideas.

3. Should students have the choice of learning Chinese, Japanese or English?
   - ▶ Why? Why not? Support your opinion.

4. Should students learn more than one foreign language in school?
   - ▶ Why? Why not? Support your opinion.

5. Are bilingual Korean teachers better than native speakers of English?
   - ▶ Why? Why not? Support your opinion.

6. Do you think Korean parents should speak in English and Korean to their children?
   - ▶ Why? Why not? Support your opinion.

7. Should English be an Official Language in Korea?
   - ▶ Why? Why not? Support your opinion.

8. What is the best way to learn a language?
   - ▶ Explain your ideas.

9. Why is it important to have many languages in the world?
   - ▶ What do you think?

10. Why are so many languages disappearing?
    - ▶ What can we do about this problem?
    - ▶ Explain your thoughts

Conversation Strategies

Making your point:		Expressing doubt:	
The point is … The thing is … The fact is … Don't forget that … What I'm saying is …	Konglish is a World English.	Yes, but … Possibly, but … What bothers me is … The problem is … I'm afraid …	that doesn't help me pass the TOEFL test.

Dialogue

- Listen to Track 72 on the CD-Rom.
- Read the dialogue with your partner.
- Perform the dialogue together.
- Change roles. Perform the dialogue again.

(Kevin is doing his homework. Mr. Brown enters the living room.)

Mr. Brown	Hello, Kevin. Why the long face?
Kevin	Hi, dad. It's my Spanish homework.
Mr. Brown	What's the problem?
Kevin	I just can't get the hang of it.
Mr. Brown	Hang in there, Kevin. It'll make sense in time.
Kevin	I don't see why I have to learn Spanish. Everybody speaks English.
Mr. Brown	Actually, more people speak Mandarin or Spanish.
Kevin	OK, dad. Everybody in America.
Mr. Brown	Wrong again, Kevin. At least 45 million don't speak English at home.
Kevin	Give me a break, dad. I don't need to learn a language.
Mr. Brown	I know it seems that way, but you'll be thankful in the end. Learning a language helps you in many ways.
Kevin	I know, I know. I've heard it all from my teacher.
Mr. Brown	It's true, Kevin.
Kevin	I just wish it wasn't so difficult.
Mr. Brown	If you can speak three languages, you'll never be out of a job.
Kevin	OK, dad. I'll do my best.
Mr. Brown	Adiós. Hasta luego!

Key Words and Expressions

long face
sad, worried expression

get the hang of it
understand; cope with

"Hang in there."
"Keep trying."
"Don't give up."

"Give me a break."
"Please understand me."
"Don't be hard on me."

"Adiós. Hasta luego!"
"Goodbye. See you later!"
(Spanish)

Dialogue Quiz

1. What is Kevin doing?
2. Why does he have a long face?
3. What does Kevin think about learning Spanish?
4. Does Kevin want to learn three languages?
5. What advice does Mr. Brown give Kevin?
6. Why does Mr. Brown say 'Adiós. Hasta luego!'?

Let's Speak a New Language! 2

- If you could speak in a different language, which one would you choose?
- Write the name of your chosen language in the box below.

Our chosen language is:

1. Now go to Google Translate: https://translate.google.com.
2. Write one of the sentences (below) in the left hand box.
3. Choose your language in the right hand box.

For example: (English to Czech)

| English | Spanish | French | English-detected ▼ | ⇄ | English | Czech | Arabic ▼ | Translate |

What's your name?   Jak se jmenuješ?

- Write the words of your chosen language in the right hand box.
- Make your own sentences for 11 to 14.

1 What's your name?
2 My name is (your name)
3 How old are you?
4 I am (your age) years old.
5 Where do you live?
6 I live in (your town).
7 What is your favorite color?
8 My favorite color is (color name).
9 What is your favorite movie?
10 My favorite movie is (movie name).
11
12
13
14

 2

- Click on the 🔊 link in Google Translate, to hear the words in your chosen language.
- Practice the pronunciation together.

Let's Teach Each Other!

1. (Pairs) Teach the other pair how to say What's your name? in your chosen language.
2. (Everyone) Teach each other how to say all the sentences.
3. See if you can have a conversation in your chosen languages.
4. You can make notes here about the other pair's sentences.

Language WordSearch

- Can you find all the languages in this WordSearch?
- Words are hidden → ↓ and ↘.
- The solution is in the Answer Section at the back of the book.

```
S U A D V F G L X V Q U Z V Y G E R
W L N Z P O R T U G U E S E E C N U
E N K G E R M A N F G I C L N A G S
D O C N F Z U C H I N E S E Q R L S
I R H A R I J A P A N E S E S A I I
S W B Q E F N H I N D I E Z I B S A
H E I X N O J N O S C K U O L I H N
A G P O C O J W I H I U T U M C M Q
Z I V Z H T J J J S S S C I C V S V
X A S P A N I S H A H W R X M N O B
C N C C Z E C H R G J N O N K D F F
F N I T A L I A N E I E A G M Z M M
```

Arabic	Chinese	Czech	English	Finnish
French	German	Hindi	Italian	Japanese
Norwegian	Portuguese	Russian	Spanish	Swedish

Konglish 143

Speaking Self-assessment

- In Unit 13 (page 112) we looked at your listening skills.
- In Unit 15 (page 128) we looked at your discussion skills.
- Let's take a look now at your conversation skills.
- What are you good at? What do you need to improve?
- Fill in your profile at the bottom of this page.

	1	2	3	4
Range	Not enough range for communication. Poor basic grammar.	Almost enough range for the task. Little control of grammar.	Just enough range for the task. Some control of grammar.	Enough range to communicate easily. Control of grammar.
Ease of Speech	Many hesitations, repetitions, single words and body gestures.	Pauses, single words and short sentences.	Connected speech, short delays. Communication OK despite errors.	No delay. Short sentences. Communication smooth.
Attitude	No enthusiasm. Lack of confidence and motivation. Nervous.	Some desire to perform the task. Lack of confidence and motivation.	Positive attitude. Confidence/ motivation/anxiety do not prevent communcation.	Positive attitude, confidence and motivation. Encourages others.
Delivery	Speech slow. No intonation. Pronunciation difficulties.	Low volume, poor intonation, poor stress and word rhythm.	Pronunciation difficulties, but delivery allows communication to continue.	No pronunciation difficulties. Delivery enhances communication.
Interaction	Speaks very little and needs help from the others. No communication strategies.	Tries to communicate. Needs help. Can communicate a little.	Sometimes needs help. Tries to interact. Shows interest in the discussion.	Actively interacts. Good body language. Encourages others.

READI Profile

- How is your profile?

	1	2	3	4
My Range				
My Ease of Speech				
My Attitude				
My Delivery				
My Interaction				

Unit 18 The Global Village

Brainstorming

- What do you know about the Global Village?
- What do you think it means?
- Let's make a flag for the Global Village.

Because of satellite communication (cell phones) and electronic mass media (radio, TV, the Internet, CDs, DVDs), time and space are growing smaller. All the different nations and races in the world can contact each other, wherever they are. This is an opportunity for people around the globe to come together in peace and cooperation.

Task 1

Making a Global Flag
- How can we show these ideas on a flag?
- Talk with your partner and fill in your design below.

Task 2

Sharing the Flag
- Show your flag to another pair of students.
- Talk about your flags together.
- What were you trying to show with your flags? How did you show it?

The Global Village

- Read this passage together and listen to Track 73.
- While you read, match the words and definitions at the bottom of the page

Marshall MacLuhan predicted the Global Village some thirty years before it became a reality. Writing in 1962, he described how the globe would be contracted into a village by electric technology. Now, more than 60 years later, his words have indeed come true. Thanks to smartphones, email, SNSs and even keypals, we can communicate with people across the world in real time, irrespective of space or national borders.

In fact the term Global Village has many meanings. For example, it is the name of a festival city in Dubai. In addition, the organization Habitat for Humanity runs a Global Village volunteer program to help homeless people, while Global Village Engineers help people in developing countries build schools, roads and hospitals.

As well as giving us the ability to read about, spread, and react immediately to global news, the Global Village is also helping individuals come closer and share their interests. We can see this on the Internet, where sites such as Care2, Grist and MySpace cater to caring communities around the globe.

In a world of huge corporations and international politics, it is easy for individual people to feel unimportant. However, the Global Village is giving us all a chance to make a difference and to work for a peaceful, unified world.

Match the words on the left to the definitions on the right.

become a reality	actual time; immediate
contracted	change from ideas to actual events
real time	home; house; dwelling; surroundings
irrespective of	large business; enterprise
habitat	made smaller
humanity	provide for
cater to	the human race; generosity; kindness
corporation	together; one
unified	without thinking about …

Further Reading: There are more reading passages at www.inkbooks.co.kr

Comprehension Check

1. Who predicted the Global Village?
2. What does 'it' (paragraph 2, line 1) refer to?
3. What does the Global Village volunteer program do?
4. What do Global Village Engineers do?
5. How is the Internet helping people come closer?
6. How can individual people make a difference in the Global Village?
7. Can you find another word for 'nations' in the passage?

Think for Yourself

- [ ] Who was Marshall MacLuhan? (Google Search)
- [ ] What is a keypal?
- [ ] Are you a member of the Global Village?

Background Information

Did you know?

- [ ] If the world were a village of 1000 people:

  ▶ There would be 584 Asians, 124 Africans, 95 Europeans, 84 Latin Americans, 55 Russians, 52 North Americans, and 6 Australians and New Zealanders.

  ▶ 165 people would speak Mandarin (Chinese).

  ▶ 86 people would speak English.

  ▶ There would be 329 Christians, 178 Moslems, 132 Hindus and 60 Buddhists.

  ▶ 330 of the people in the village would be children.

  ▶ Sixty people would be over 65.

  ▶ The population in the next year would be 1018.

  ▶ Only 70 people would own a car.

  ▶ About 33% would not have clean, safe drinking water.

  ▶ There would be 5 soldiers, 7 teachers and 1 doctor.

Discussion   Us ▸ Groups

- Talk about the questions below.
- Use the **Conversation Strategies** at the bottom of the page.

1 Has globalization affected your life?
  ▸ Explain your opinion.

2 Has the Global Village improved our lives?
  ▸ Defend your ideas.

3 How can the Global Village make the world a better place?
  ▸ Discuss together and support your opinion.

4 What are the advantages of globalization?
  ▸ Discuss together and support your opinion.

5 What are the disadvantages of globalization?
  ▸ Discuss together and support your opinion.

6 Do you think the Global Village will destroy national borders?
  ▸ Why? Why not? Explain your ideas.

7 Will globalization make everyone the same?
  ▸ Describe your thoughts.

8 Is the Global Village destroying local cultures?
  ▸ Explain your ideas.

9 Is the Global Village destroying local languages?
  ▸ Explain your ideas.

10 What will the Global Village look like in 50 years?
  ▸ Support your opinion.

Conversation Strategies

	Pausing for thought:	Looking for the right words:	
What do you think of the Global Village?	Let me see. Let me think. That's a good question. I'd like to think about that. I'll get back to you on that.	Let me just say, Let me put it this way, How shall I put it? How can I say this? What shall I say?	I think it's a great opportunity for international peace and cooperation.

Dialogue

- Listen to Track 74 on the CD-Rom.
- Read the dialogue with your partner.
- Perform the dialogue together.
- Change roles. Perform the dialogue again.

(Mr. Brown is watching the Evening News on TV.)

Kevin	Hello, dad. Anything interesting on TV?
Mr. Brown	Not much, Kevin. The news seems all the same these days.
Kevin	I know. War, terrorism, extreme weather …
Mr. Brown	But I saw something about globalization and the Global Village.
Kevin	Oh, yes? What was it?
Mr. Brown	You know how the world is getting smaller due to EM?
Kevin	Of course. We studied it in school.
Mr. Brown	Only corporations and politicians have been interested up to now.
Kevin	You mean FTAs and other things?
Mr. Brown	That's right. For you and me, it was all pie in the sky.
Kevin	You're not kidding. Globalization is for CEOs.
Mr. Brown	Well, it seems things are changing, thanks to the Internet.
Kevin	Really? How's that?
Mr. Brown	People are making GICs and sharing their ideas.
Kevin	You mean we can speak with anyone around the world?
Mr. Brown	Yes. Ordinary people are becoming important at last.
Kevin	Wow. The Global Village is cool.

Key Words and Expressions

extreme weather
typhoons, hurricanes, floods, droughts

EM
electronic media

FTA
Free Trade Agreement

pie in the sky
an impossible dream

CEO
Chief Executive Officer; Head of a company

GIC
Global Internet Community

Dialogue Quiz

1. What is the usual content of the Evening News?
2. How was it different tonight?
3. What effect is electronic mass media having on the world?
4. How do GICs help people?
5. Why does Kevin say the Global Village is cool?

Trivia game: Ideas

- Did you read the Background Information in each Unit (pages 11, 19, 27, … 147)?
- Let's make a Trivia Game based on that information.

Task 1 — Choose 5 items of Background Information from different Units. Write them in the boxes.

1.

2.

3.

4.

5.

Task 2 — Change the statements into 'Wh' questions or 'How' questions. For example:
Statement: 'The Busan International Film Festival started in 1996.' (page 27)
Question: 'When did the Busan Film Festival start?'

1.

2.

3.

4.

5.

Our Questions Us Groups

- Talk about your questions with your group members.
- Rank your questions according to their difficulty (100, 50, 20 and 10 points).

100	50	20	10

Write the numbers of your questions in the grid. For example, perhaps Q1 is worth 20 points. Maybe Q2 is worth 50 points, etc.

Now Let's play the Trivia Game! (2 groups)

Group A
1: Ask group B for a question.
3: If your answer is correct, write your score in the box below (on the left).

Group B
2: Read the question that group A asked for.
4: If group A answers correctly, write their score in the box below (on the right).
If group A answers incorrectly, they get no score.

Group B
1: Ask group A for a question.
3: If your answer is correct, write your score in the box below (on the left).

Group A
2: Read the question that group B asked for.
4: If group B answers correctly, write their score in the box below (on the right).
If group B answers incorrectly, they get no score.

Continue asking questions until all 20 questions have been read out.

Our scores:

100	50	20	10

Our opponents' scores:

100	50	20	10

The Global Village 151

Reflect and Review

- We have come to the final page.
- It's time to look back on what we have learned.
- It's also time to look forward to what we will do next.

Task 1 Fill in this reflection survey.
Remember, there are no correct answers.
Just say what you mean and mean what you say!

1	Which was your favorite Unit?	
2	Which was your least favorite Unit?	
3	Which was your favorite reading passage?	
4	Which was your favorite discussion?	
5	Which was your favorite role-play?	
6	Which was your favorite debate?	
7	What did you learn from this book?	
8	What are you better at now?	
9	What do you still need to improve?	
10	What are your future plans for studying?	
11	What are your goals for the future?	
12	How will you achieve those goals?	

Answer Key

Who's Who?
Page 8

Helen's husband is called Michael. Helen's mother-in-law is called grandma Brown. Helen is Michael's wife. Kevin's friend is Park Seung-min. Jenny's brother, Kevin, is Seung-min's friend. Jenny is Helen's daughter and Ji-hye's friend.

Unit 1
Page 9

Here is the solution to the Friendship Test:

1. This number is your favorite number!
2. This is the number of your closest friends.
3. This is the person you love.
4. This is the person you care most about.
5. This person knows you very well.
6. This person brings you luck.
7. You like this person, but sometimes it is difficult to understand him/her.
8. This song matches the person in number 3.
9. This song is for the person in 7.
10. This song tells you about your mind.
11. This song tells you how you feel about life.

Unit 2
Page 24

Here is the solution to the Favorite Color puzzle:

Name:	Mary	Peter	John	Jane
Favorite color:	Yellow	Blue	Red	Green

Unit 5
Page 41

Here are some possible answers to the Feelings Task.

Answer Key

Unit 6
Page 49

Here are the answers to the Food Crossword.

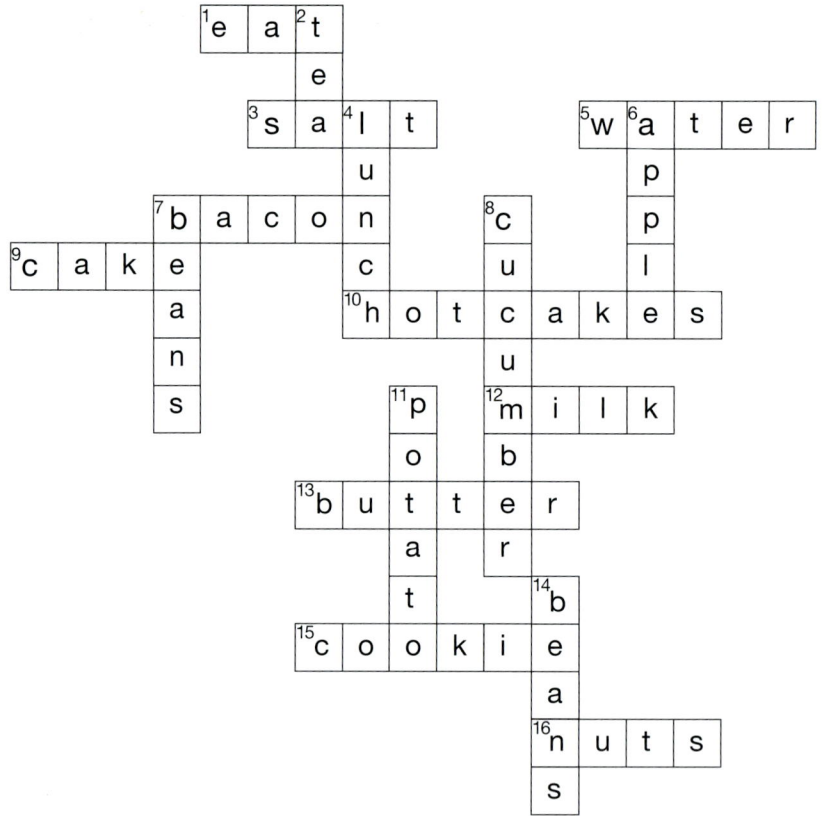

Unit 10
Page 81

Here are the answers to the Traffic WordSearch.

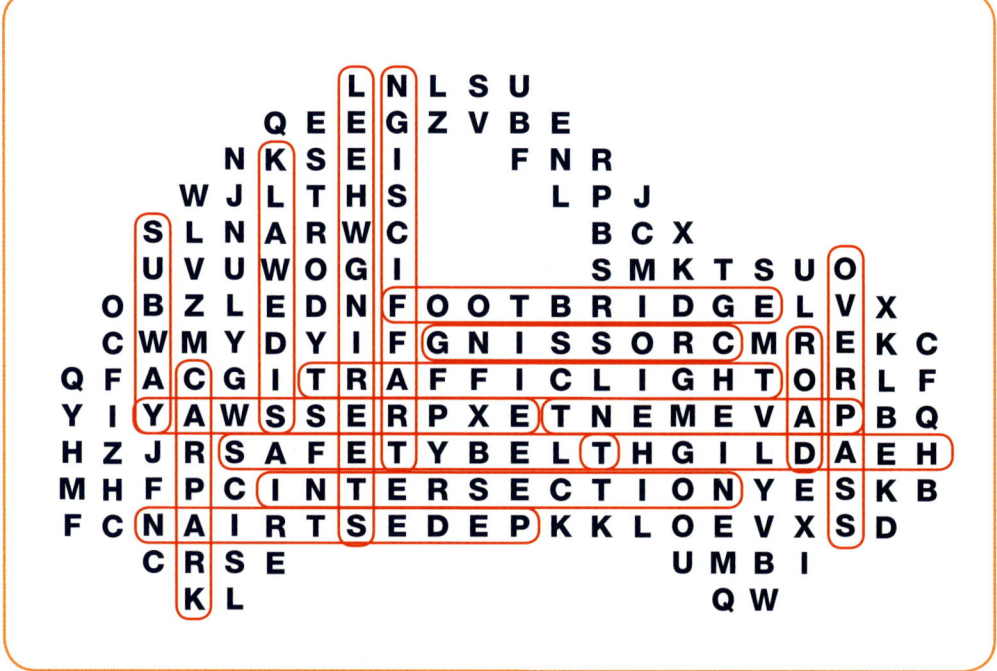

Answer Key

Unit 10
Page 88

Here is a solution to the Car Park Puzzle. Every vehicle has to be moved.

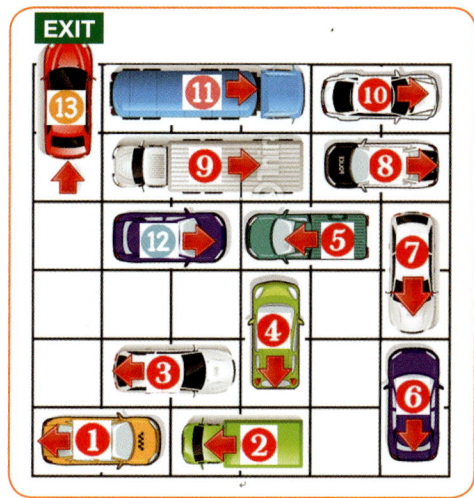

Unit 11
Page 96

Here are the solutions to the brain teasers.

Puzzle 1: The last person took the basket as well as the apple!

Puzzle 2: The surgeon is the boy's mother.

Puzzle 3: The chances of the coin coming down tails are still 50%. The coin has no memory of what happened before.

Puzzle 4: The man is a dwarf. He cannot reach the button for the 18th floor.

Or: The man likes walking up the stairs for exercise (but not too many stairs!).

Puzzle 5: The best way to solve this puzzle is to think of where the money is now:
- There is $25 in the cash register.
- There is $2 in the waiter's pocket.
- There is $1 in the pocket of each person.
- 25 + 2 + 1 + 1 + 1 = $30.

Unit 12
Page 97

Here are the answers to the vocabulary matching activity (Task 1).

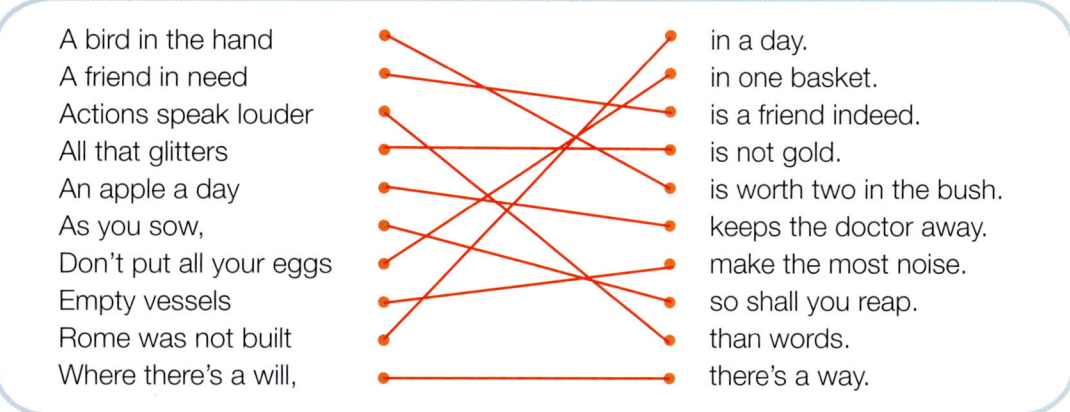

Answer Key 155

Answer Key

Unit 12
Page 97

Here are the answers to Task 2.

Don't put all your eggs in one basket.
(Don't put all your hopes on one thing. Have a backup plan.)

Actions speak louder than words.
(Anyone can talk, but it's what you do that counts.)

Where there's a will, there's a way.
(If you really want to do something, you will find a way of doing it.)

A friend in need is a friend indeed.
(A real friend is someone who helps you when you are in trouble.)

Empty vessels make the most noise.
(People who don't know much do the most talking.)

A bird in the hand is worth two in the bush.
(Hold on to what you have, instead of going after something that looks better.)

Unit 12
Page 101

Here are the meanings of the Scottish proverbs.

'A black hen lays a white egg.'
➡ Don't judge people by their looks. Appearance isn't everything. Things are not always what they seem.

'What may be done at any time will be done at no time.'
➡ If you leave things to be done some time in the future, you will probably never do them.

Unit 12
Page 104

Here are the hidden proverbs.

When in Rome, do as the Romans do.
Every cloud has a silver lining.
Don't judge a book by its cover.
Make hay while the sun shines.
Two wrongs don't make a right.
There's no place like home.
Practice make perfect.
Better late than never.
Love is blind.
Walls have ears.
Birds of a feather flock together.
Two heads are better than one.
The early bird catches the worm.

Answer Key

Unit 13
Page 105

Here are the dates of the headlines.

- April 16, 1912: The Titanic sinks 4 hours after being it by an iceberg.
- October 25, 1929 (Black Tuesday): The Biggest Wall Street crash ever.
- July 30, 1966: England wins the World Cup.
- April 4, 1968: Martin Luther King is shot in Memphis.
- July 21, 1969: American Neil Armstrong becomes the first man to walk on the Moon.
- August 31, 1997: Lady Diana, the ex-wife of Prince Charles of the UK, is killed in a car crash in Paris.
- September 11, 2001: The Twin Towers (World Trade Centre) collapse in New York.
- December 14, 2006: Ban Ki-moon becomes Secretary General of the United Nations.
- February 25, 2010: Kim Yuna wins the Figure Skating Gold Medal in the Winter Olympics.

Unit 15
Page 121

Here are the answers to the Relationships crossword.

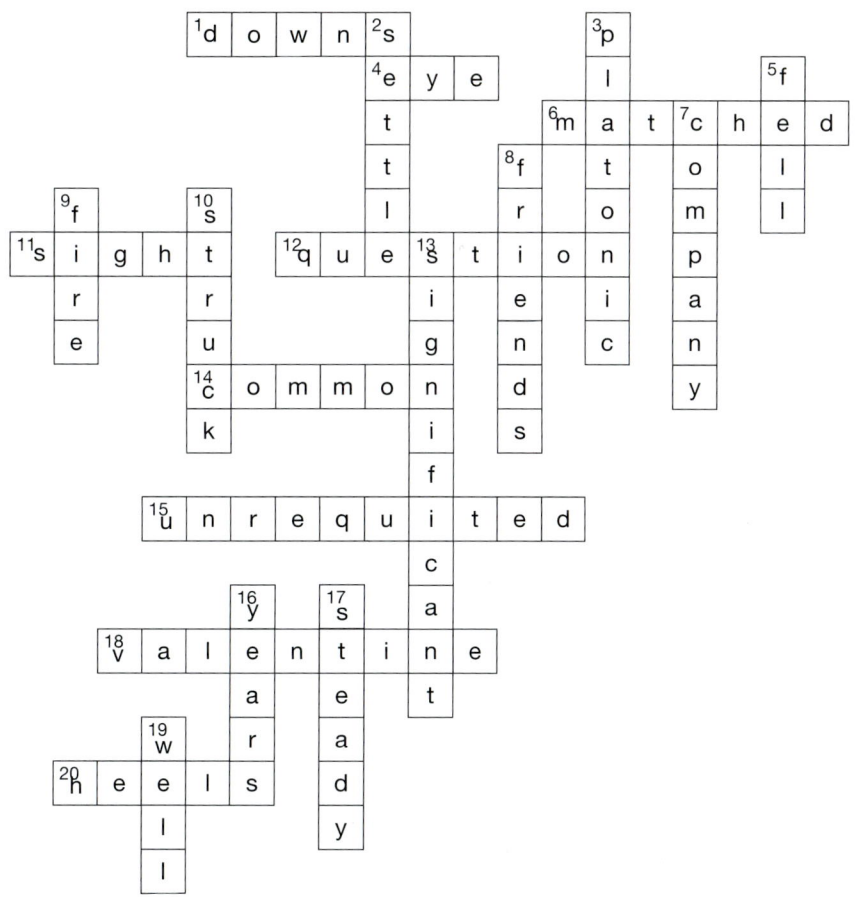

Answer Key

Unit 16 — Page 129

Here are the answers to the Inventions-Matching task.

Rank	Inventions	Descriptions
___	Penicillin	This gives us a network of communication.
___	The Television	This puts words on the page.
___	The Automobile	This performs calculations very quickly.
___	The Camera	This gives us entertainment in our homes.
___	The Computer	This captures images.
___	The Printing Press	This is a method of private transport.
___	The Light Bulb	This changes electricity into light.
___	The Internet	This transmits your voice.
___	The Steam Engine	This cures infections and diseases.
___	The Telephone	This powered the first trains.

Unit 16 — Page 129

Here are some suggestions for the Alphabetical Inventions Task.

Air Balloon	Bicycle	Computer	Diesel Engine
Eiffel Tower	Film	Glue	Helicopter
Ice cream	Jet Aircraft	Keyboard	Laser Printer
Microscope	Nail Polish	Overcoat	Paper Clip
QWERTY	Radio	Sandwich	Telegraph
Umbrella	Volleyball	Watches	X-Rays
YouTube	Zipper		

Unit 16 — Page 136

Here are the answers to the Save The World Puzzle.

reduce reuse recycle

save water
every drop counts

plant a tree
plant a life

switch off
save energy

save the earth

There's no place like home!

158 Active English Discussion 2

Answer Key

Unit 17
Page 137

Here are the World Englishes and their countries.

- Banglish Bangladesh
- Chinglish China
- Finglish Finland
- Franglaish France
- Inglish India
- Italglish Italy
- Japlish Japan
- Manglish Malaysia
- Paklish Pakistan
- Runglish Russia
- Shanglish Shanghai
- Singlish Singapore
- Spanglish Spain
- Thaiglish Thailand
- Wenglish Wales

Unit 17
Page 143

Here is the solution to the Language WordSearch.

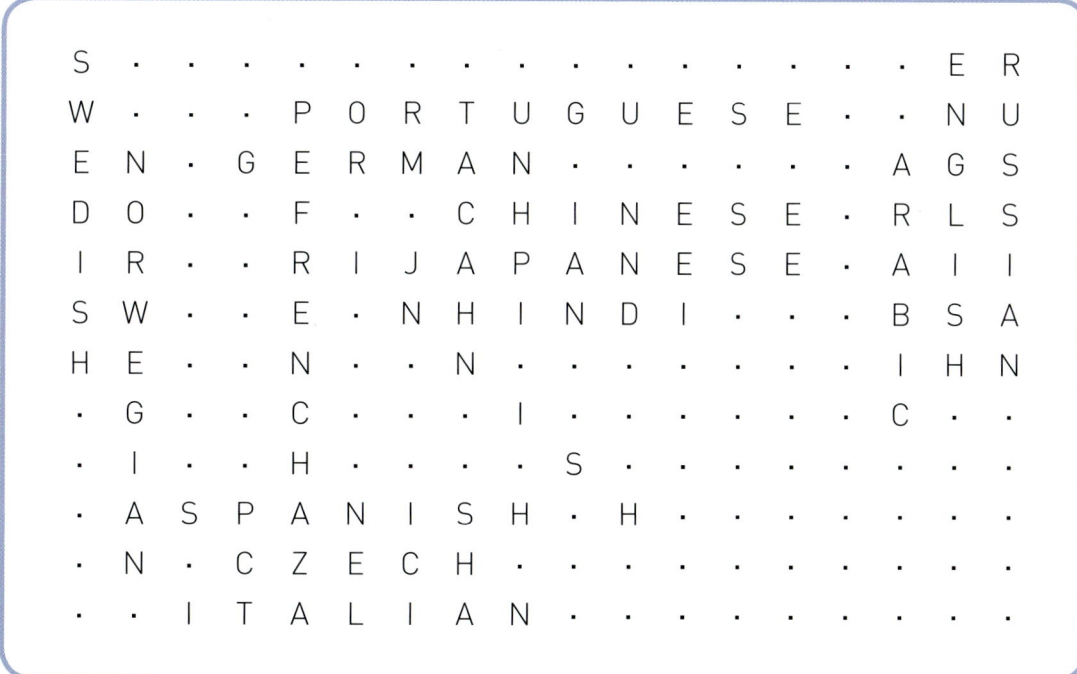